JEFF PENNANT'S
Field Guide
TO
RAISING HAPPY PARENTS

Kelli McKinney

CHICKEN SCRATCH BOOKS
WWW.CHICKENSCRATCHBOOKS.COM

Text Copyright © 2022 by Kelli McKinney
Cover Art Copyright © 2022 by Wyndham Batton

All rights reserved. No part of this publication may be reproduced, distributed or transmitted in any form or by any means, including photocopying, recording, or other electronic or mechanical methods, without the prior written permission of the publisher, except in the case of brief quotations embodied in critical reviews and certain other noncommercial uses permitted by copyright law. For permission requests, write to the publisher, addressed "Attention: Permissions Coordinator," at the address below.

Chicken Scratch Books

PO Box 104

Wisdom, MT 59761

www.chickenscratchbooks.com

Publisher's Note: This is a work of fiction. Names, characters, places, and incidents are a product of the author's imagination. Locales and public names are sometimes used for atmospheric purposes. Any resemblance to actual people, living or dead, or to businesses, companies, events, institutions, or locales is completely coincidental.

Ordering Information: Special discounts are available on quantity purchases by corporations, associations, and others. For details, contact the publisher at the address above.

First Chicken Scratch Books Printing, 2022

ISBN 978-1-953743-18-3 (paperback)

ISBN 978-1-953743-19-0 (ebook)

Printed in the United States of America

*For David and Aidan,
my forever team*

Chapter 1

No way am I taking my eyes off this screen. After three weeks of work, I finally—finally!—make it to the last boss battle in Fire Ant Heroes 3. So yeah, even though my dog Zip just puked pizza crust on the carpet, that mess is going to have to wait.

I am about to become a legend.

It's about time, too. You know GamerCon, right? It's only the most epic gamer convention ever and it's coming here in three weeks. Me and my best friends Evan Graham and Quenton Maxwell are going. It's going to be next-level awesome. We might even enter a tournament, that's how awesome it'll be.

Fire Ant Heroes 3 is pretty much the best game out there. Evan's an expert-level wingman and Q's the most reliable healer I've ever seen. Me? Unless Zip manages to barf on my controller, I'm about to level up to expert warrior status.

We've been working on this forever. Once I level up, all three of us will be at the top of our game. We'll be an unstoppable team.

Right now, I'm using antennae lasers against two ridiculously overpowered armadillos and it's totally working. They're down to like, 18 percent health. It's getting ugly in here. For them. Victory is so close that I have to bounce on the couch with each laser blast.

But then this happens.

"Jeffrey Thomas Pennant, what did I tell you about screen time?"

Mom's home. Out of the corner of my eye, I see her approach from the entryway. The armadillos are at nine percent health. I'm almost there. I mash the controller buttons like my life depends on it. Because it kind of does.

I feel Mom's stare, but I can't stop now. Must. Level. Up. *Eight percent.*

She picks up the tv remote.

"No-no-no-NO-NO—"

Click.

"NOOOOOOOOO! I was so close!" I flop face down on the couch and yell into the cushions. "This is so unfair! Do you know what you just did?"

"Answer my question, please. We talked about it this morning. What did I say?"

"Ymmph smmmph chmmph fmmph." I mutter into the couch. What's she even doing here? She's never home from work this early.

All my hard work. Destroyed by Mom's thumb.

"Please sit up."

She's so calm about ruining my life.

I groan and prop myself up on my elbows. "I was in the middle of a boss fight. You know how I feel about boss fights."

Mom perches on the arm of the couch. "Mhm. And *you* know how *I* feel about listening. What did I say this morning about screen time?" It's clear she doesn't care about my pain.

"You said 'chores first.'"

"That's right. And that means what, exactly?"

I push myself upright and sigh. Yeah. I know what 'chores first' means. What I don't remember, exactly, is what my chores actually are. "Ummm...."

"Take out the trash. Empty the dishwasher. When you're done, and when you've done your homework, then you can play." She stands, then lightning-fast she leans over and smooches the top of my head. "Oh. And clean up the dog mess, please. Thank you, pumpkin."

"*Mom*. I'm in fifth grade. I'm nobody's pumpkin!" It's no use. She's already halfway down the hall.

The good news is I don't have homework today. Ha. So the only things standing in between me and those armadillos are trash and a full dishwasher.

I leap off the couch and land splat in a squishy, warm pile of goo. Oh, yeah. I gotta clean up Zip's mess too. This stinks. I hop into the kitchen and rinse my gooey foot in the sink, then I guess it's chore time. No thanks to Mom.

In a flash, I scrub the carpet clean, wash my hands,

and take the clean dishes out of the dishwasher.

Look at that. One chore down in record time. What's next? Taking out the trash. Uggggh. I need speed and power, and I need it now.

That can only mean one thing.

I run to the hall closet and grab Big Tex, my ginormous radio-controlled monster truck, and its mini-remote. If I absolutely have to do chores, might as well make them fast and fun, right?

I power up, race back to the kitchen, and park Big Tex next to the garbage bin like a boss. It only takes one heave to hoist the full trash bag out, then PLOP! I drop it into the truck bed. Not too shabby. So what if half the bag hangs off the back bumper? Who has time to be picky? I gotta get these chores d-o-n-e if I want to have time to level up before dinner.

Next stop: The bathroom that my big sister Sadie and I share. I steer Tex down the hall like it's a racetrack straightaway. Once Tex hits the bathroom door, we're all business. Park. Heave. Pack. Drive. What's my secret to getting it done so quickly? I stuff the bathroom trash bag inside the kitchen trash. Genius move, I know.

This is working great! Time to kick things up a notch.

Can Big Tex and I deliver all the garbage to the garage in less than three minutes? It's the ultimate test of Big Tex's strength and my ingenuity.

Two words: Can. Do.

I check my watch and note the starting time. Count

down: 3-2-1! Punch the accelerator. Big Tex is dripping greasy brown fluid, but that's fine. Totally fine. I'll take care of it later.

One last Park. Heave. Pack. And then it's go, Tex, go!

We zoom down the hall and whoops those skid marks on the wall will come off with a little warm water. Probably.

We blitz into the garage with fifteen seconds to spare.

It's up to me to finish the job. Prepare, one and all, for the spectacular finale. I can almost hear the crowd chanting *Jeff! Jeff! Jeff!* I grab Big Tex's overstuffed payload in one hand and thrust it into the air, then slam the trash bag into the can and take a bow.

Thank you, why yes, that was a world record. No autographs, please.

From somewhere in the house, I hear my name. For real. Out loud and everything. "Jeff?"

"Yeah?"

"Please come here."

Full of victory, Big Tex and I cruise toward the kitchen. I bet Mom is waiting there with a congratulatory snack. I mean, I did just finish my chores in record time. That's gotta be worth some fruit snacks or something.

Mom's sitting at the table. Used paper and plastic products are scattered in front of her. But there's no sign of snacky goodness anywhere.

"Have a seat." She points me to a chair directly across from her. I set Big Tex on the floor and do what she says. "Why did I find a trail of trash across the house? Why is it not in the garbage can in the garage?"

What is she talking about? "It's not. I mean, it is. I just took out a giant bag of garbage. I'm done. Can I play my game now?"

She ignores my question and plucks a wrinkly piece of aluminum foil from the table. "This was in my room. How'd it get there?"

Huh. Not sure how I'd know that. I was busy making up a pretty sweet monster truck game. "I don't know. I didn't go in there, it's your personal space."

"So how did trash get into my personal space? I don't leave trash in your room, do I?"

"Um, no. We have a deal." I stay out of Mom and Dad's room. They stay out of mine. There's even a great big sign on my door that says NO PARENTS PAST THIS POINT.

I shrug. "Maybe Zip took it in there. I really don't know. Hey, want to see how I used Big Tex to take the trash out? It's actually pretty awesome."

"Maybe in a minute. You weren't paying very close attention to your work, were you?" Mom points to a syrupy blob near the garbage bin.

"Where did that come from?" Then I remember. That's the brown gunk that dribbled out of the bag when I loaded it onto Big Tex.

Zip's "Dad's home" bark bellows across the house. Mom glances at her watch. "Is it six already?"

Oh man. If Mom doesn't hurry up and make her point, there's no way I'm getting another round of FAH3 in before dinner.

"Why the city decides to close an on-ramp during rush hour, I'll never understand." Dad kisses the top of my head, then Mom's.

Whenever it's Dad's turn to make dinner, count on four servings of the Gino's Deli daily special. It must be Dad's turn because I smell Gino's. Sure enough—Dad opens the fridge and plonks two giant paper takeout bags inside, then sits next to Mom. "Mom texted me and said you'd had an interesting afternoon. Want to tell your side of the story?"

Story? What story? "Wait. Am I in trouble?"

"Your mom told you no screen time until your chores and homework are done. Right? But what were you doing when Mom came home?"

I'm confused. What's the problem, exactly? I look at Mom. "Well, I forgot at first, but—I mean, we talked about it, right Mom? You reminded me and I did my chores."

"You did your chores *halfway,* Jeff," Mom says. "You left the dishes on the counter."

"You said 'empty the dishwasher.' It's empty." I grab the edge of the table. "Dad. You always say it's important to be factually accurate. I emptied the dishwasher. Factually accurate."

Mom leans forward. "You left trash everywhere."

"You said 'take out the trash' so I took out the trash! I didn't know that other stuff happened. I'll pick up the stuff that fell out, okay? I didn't know!"

Dad grabs a napkin and waves it like a referee flag. "That's enough arguing, Jeff. I think Mom is trying to tell you that you need to do your chores right the first time."

"I did exactly what she said."

"We'll agree to disagree on that," Mom says. "There are four of us living here, so all four of us need to help out. If one of us doesn't do our part, what happens? Someone else has to pick up the slack. Is that fair?"

"Pennants don't do things halfway," Dad says.

"Fine, I get it, I get it." I scooch my chair backward.

"I'm not convinced that you do," Mom says. "It's time to step up your game, son. I think we need another day without screen time to make sure you hear us."

"NO! Please. I hear you. I promise. I'll do better."

"I know you will, but the answer is still 'no.' No screens until Saturday morning." Mom walks to the sink and washes her hands.

I feel like I've been elbowed in the throat.

As if that's not bad enough, Dad swoops in with the finishing blow. "And, you need to put the dishes away and pick up the trash you dropped. Before dinner."

I stand up and push my chair back. "This isn't fair. You always say 'you're only a kid once, appreciate childhood.' Don't you? Live my best life, right?"

"That's right." Mom dries her hands on a towel that says 'Live. Love. Laugh.' So I know she knows what I'm talking about.

"Well, tell me this: What do chores have to do with

living your best life?"

Mom says nothing. She pats the top of my head and walks out of the kitchen.

"Dad?"

"Nothing halfway, buddy." He smiles and leaves.

I can't believe this. Now I'm going to have to wait a whole day before I level up.

I don't even know where half these dishes go, but I manage to get the countertop cleared off and the trash pile dumped into the bin.

By the time Sadie gets home from dance class and we sit down for dinner, I'm feeling a little better.

I mean, yeah, I wish I could have completed my boss fight. And I wish I could play tomorrow. But it's only 24 hours. I'll still have time to level up. We'll still be unstoppable. I mean, Evan, Q, and I are best friends for life, no matter what level we are.

This is just a little parent-shaped pause in my progress.

Chapter 2

After Science Club, Evan's riding the bus home with Q. Since Q lives across the street from me, that means Evan's riding the bus home with me too.

So today, thanks to Evan's mom, the ride home on bus 10 is full of awesome.

The three of us share a bench seat and watch YouTube on Evan's phone. "Did you guys see this one?" Evan tilts his phone sideways so *Epic Science Fails* fills the full screen. "Watch this kid right here." On screen, a guy in an oversized lab coat fills an empty water bottle about halfway with vinegar.

"He's got that wrong. Totally wrong." Q's glasses slide down his nose. "That's too much vinegar for a bottle that size."

"I know, right?" Evan says. "It's like he's trying to fail."

"It could work, though, couldn't it?" I touch the screen to pause. "It might actually."

Evan slumps in the seat. "No dude, just no. You haven't seen this. Watch. It's hilarious. The kid cries at the end."

"Um, spoiler alert." Q nudges Evan's elbow.

"Hang on." I grab the phone and hold it out of Evan's reach. "If he uses enough baking soda, I bet that kid's rocket flies 25 feet. At least."

Evan scoffs. "Whatever."

"Not 'whatever,' it's totally possible. I mean, *I* could do it." I waggle my eyebrows because I'm right. "I could build a bottle rocket that goes at least that far."

"There's no way. Not with a bottle that small." Evan turns around in his seat and leans against the window, still facing me.

"You don't think I can do it? What about you, Q?"

"Best case? A bottle that size could go about fifteen feet. I know you can't do it." Q says. "Come on. Just give him his phone and let's finish the video."

"I'll bet you. I bet you five bucks I can make a bottle rocket that flies at least 25 feet."

Evan and Q sit taller. "Five bucks each?" Q asks.

"Five bucks each."

"Dude, you are so on." Evan extends a hand.

We've handshaked on it. There's no going back.

When the bus pulls up at Q's and my stop, we pile out and head straight to my house. Evan and Q dig through the recycle bin for empty bottles, while I raid the pantry.

We pile all the supplies on the kitchen table: Pencils, tape, markers, measuring cups, empty water bottles, baking soda, and vinegar. We're super quick because we know what we're doing. Next to video games and YouTube, science is kind of our thing. We've won the Franklin Pierce Elementary School Science Fair two years in a row.

"Wait." Q counts the gear. "We have enough supplies. Why don't we each build one? Then we can see whose rocket travels the farthest?" Q asks.

"Yeah. We should all build one," Evan chimes in.

"Let's go." I grab one of the empty bottles.

We begin construction. Soon, three small bottle rockets rest on the kitchen table. My rocket has J-E-F-F printed in orange marker down the side. Q's rocket—big surprise—has a giant purple Q on the top. Evan's is the most random. He drew a soccer ball on his rocket. We don't even play soccer—how funny is that?

The secret with bottle rockets—at least the baking soda and vinegar kind, anyway—is to make a big enough chemical reaction to create a whole bunch of thrust. That's why fuel preparation is super important.

We each take a turn with the giant vinegar jug. Evan fills his bottle halfway. Q pours about an inch into his rocket. Me? I go all in. By the time I finish, there's only about two inches of air left at the top of the bottle.

Evan piles two tablespoons of baking soda onto a paper towel and folds it up into a neat packet. Q's packet is about half the size of Evan's. I measure a quarter cup of the powdery stuff and roll it into a paper towel to form a tube.

Between the nearly-full bottle of vinegar and the pile of baking soda, I've got more fuel than both my competitors combined. It's like my dad said, right? *Pennants don't do anything halfway.* There's no way I'm going to lose this bet.

He'd be so proud.

"Ready?' Evan holds his hand palm up over the table. Q and I do the same. "Set?" We nod. "Launch!"

We slide our baking soda packets into the bottles of vinegar at the same time.

"Wait-wait-wait!" Q shrieks and waves his arms over his head like he's flagging down a plane. "We forgot—"

A thick jet of foamy, stinky liquid blasts the kitchen ceiling. It's like a snowstorm and a fire extinguisher and a skunk crashed into each other. I mean, it sprays everywhere. It doesn't smell great, but it's probably the most glorious thing I've ever seen.

I wish I was recording this.

Bubbles drip from Q's glasses. "Bottlecaps. We forgot to cap the bottles. The thrust is going the wrong direction." He crouches beneath the kitchen table.

"Ha! This is awesome!" I dance in the clumps of foamy rain. I bend down and flick a wad of goop off of Q's shoulder. "So cool! Did you see that?"

Evan lunges across the table for his gurgling, fizzy bottle. "The sink! Put them in the sink!" As soon as he touches the bottle, it belches foam all over his hands and shirt. "Aaaaaaaaaggghh!"

Then, get this—he *drops* the bottle, and it's still going! Classic! It shoots across the floor like a little plastic speed skater, straight into the fridge door. It spins, slowly, splurting out a huge puddle of white, gooey foam.

"Aww, Q. I think yours is dead." I poke his bottle. It's oozing tiny bubbles, but that's about it. Rest In Peace. Then I get an idea. I lay on the floor and flap my arms and legs. "Check it out, you guys. Snow angels."

Evan groans. Q gets his phone out and snaps photos. "Actually, we didn't make snow. That's sodium acetate." Leave it to Q to get technical.

Sadie's voice makes the three of us jump. "What did you guys do?"

When did my big sister get home? I sit up to see her standing on a patch of dry tile. "Hey Sade. We did a science."

"Is that what this is?" She makes a sour face. "Science smells like old Easter eggs." She tiptoes over to the towel drawer. "Q, your mom is outside looking for you guys."

"Oh, shoot, I forgot to text her!" Q scrambles to his feet. Which is hard to do when you're sitting in vinegar and bubbles. "See ya, Jeff."

"Later," Evan says.

They bolt out of the kitchen. "You owe me five bucks!" I shout after them. "Both of you!"

"You better get this cleaned up before Mom and Dad get home." Sadie hands me a pair of dishrags, then exits the kitchen.

I spin around and survey the damage. Except for the spongy-looking stalactites dangling from the ceiling, most of the foam has fizzled out. Vinegar puddles and a weird white powder cover the table. And the floor. Oh—and the countertops too. Yikes.

Well, Dad says to give things a hundred percent. Judging by the aftermath alone, I think I get an A-plus for my rocket-slash-volcano building.

I climb onto the kitchen table and wipe it dry. Then one of the monster gloop-sicles plops from the ceiling directly onto my head and I yelp.

And *of course*, that's when Mom and Dad walk in.

Mom leans against the wall. Dad glances at me, walks to the fridge, digs out a cold diet soda, and cracks it open. He offers it to Mom, but she shakes her head.

Dad takes a long swig. "Explain, please. *Wait*. First, get off of the table. Then explain."

When you add it all up, I've probably spent at least a full year's worth of my life explaining myself to my parents. "We wanted to see whose bottle rocket could fly the farthest."

"Who is *we*?" Mom asks.

"Evan and Q came over after school. Just for a little while."

"You made bottle rockets in the kitchen?" Dad asks.

"Nah. We meant to but turns out we made volcanos. My volcano totally dominated. It was amazing. I gave it a hundred percent, Dad. You should have seen it."

"Oh, I can see it alright."

"But I'm cleaning it up. Don't worry."

"What happened to our house rule? 'No friends over

without Mom or Dad at home?'" Dad asks.

Oh. Yeah. That one. "They weren't here very long, I promise."

Mom clears her throat. "And how about your friends? Did they have permission to come over?"

"I don't know. Maybe they don't have to ask?"

She covers her face with her hands. She inhales and exhales so loud I can hear it from over here. When she moves her hands, her face is red. "How many times do your dad and I have to repeat the same things before you listen? Nobody comes over unless Mom or Dad is at home. It's not safe."

"O-kay. I know." How do I explain the importance of a bet between best friends? Not just any bet. But a bet that I will most absolutely, certainly win? One look at Mom's robotic expression tells me she will never understand. "It's complicated."

"I see," Mom says. "Well, we have a problem. Following house rules shouldn't be so complicated. For the next week, you are grounded. No video games, no going to Q's or Evan's, and no phone after school. Maybe that will help you clear your head."

"Wait. So I can't do anything? Like, at all?"

"You can clean the kitchen." Dad hands me the mop.

"What about Q's sleepover tomorrow night?"

"You're grounded," Mom says. "Q will understand. Maybe next time you'll make better choices."

They walk out before I can say anything else. So I'm

standing alone in the kitchen with a mop, a soggy shirt, and a bunch of unsaid words swirling around inside my head.

It's so unfair. I can't be grounded for having friends over and having fun. How am I going to practice for GamerCon if I can't use screens? How am I going to keep up with my friends if I can't text?

I'm over here being 11, living my best life, and they want to talk about choices?

Why does everything have to be so hard?

Chapter 3

Allow me to state the obvious: Being grounded stinks. Tonight, Q's having a sleepover. And I'm stuck here. Not having a sleepover.

Like, it super stinks. I'm a resourceful guy, though, so I'm making a list of things I can do while I'm grounded.

1) Build a go-kart.
2) ?

I admit that this is a short list so far.

My grandparents gave me a build-your-own go-kart kit for Christmas. Cool, right?

If it's so cool, why haven't I built it yet?

Because the kit didn't include an engine. Grandma and Pops thought I'd want to choose the engine with Mom and Dad.

What's the point of having a go-kart if it doesn't, you know, go? Without an engine, a go-kart is pretty much a giant toddler toy. Who wants to waste time on a toddler toy when there are so many video games to play or YouTube to watch?

Mom and Dad disagree.

But still. If I'm not allowed to do anything *actually* cool, I might as well build my powerless push car. Who knows? After I build it, maybe Mom and Dad will change their mind. Maybe they'll feel bad. You know, when they see me pushing the kart around the block with my own two feet like a chump.

They'll say "Son, you worked really hard to build this. You're right, it does need an engine." And I'll be like, "Whaaat?!" Then they'll go, "We're sorry we were so wrong," and boom! They'll buy me an engine. I mean, that's what a normal parent would do, isn't it?

I feel like this is a foolproof plan.

So I head out to the garage. In the corner, there's a huge wooden crate, taller than me, propped up against the wall. I fish a flathead screwdriver out of Dad's toolbox and pry the lid open.

Oh man. That's a lot of parts.

We're talking not one, not two, but three bags of bolts; probably 27 orange metal pipes in who knows how many sizes, four knobby tires, a whole bunch of chains, a few feet of wire cable, a steering wheel, and a little chair that I assume is the seat.

You know what I don't see? Instructions.

On the one hand, this kart's just a life-size Lego set. I love Legos.

But on the other hand, that's seriously a lot of parts. And no engine.

How much more fun would this be if Evan and Q came over and helped me build it?

About a thousand times more fun.

Sigh.

I shove the lid back on the crate and go back to my list. I'm a smart guy. I can think of something else to do.

2)   Write haikus

Fun fact about me—but don't tell anybody—I'm kind of good at poetry. Not, you know, good enough to write a whole book. But not too shabby for a dude in fifth grade.

My favorite poems are *haikus*. They're Japanese poems in a pattern. Five syllables, then seven, then five again. I like dumping my thoughts onto paper. It's a lot like dumping baking soda into vinegar and seeing what happens (hint: amazingness).

Zip barks even before I hear Mrs. St. John's giant old car glurg up the driveway. Sadie's home. She spots me sitting in the garage and comes over, twirling her toe shoes by their ribbons like a dirty, pink lasso. "What 'cha doing?"

I twiddle the pen between my fingers. "Writing."

"Cool. Want to watch a movie with me after dinner tonight?"

"Can't. Grounded from screens."

"Still? Bummer. Think Mom and Dad will make an exception, you know, for family movie time?" She musses my hair as she walks past me.

"Um, have you met our parents? That's about as likely as Sergeant Sting joining the Waterbug Battalion."

"I have no idea what that means. But it's cool. Another time." She closes the door behind her. I click my pen and *haiku*.

> Sadie takes ballet
> But she stomps like a T-rex
> Whomp! Whomp! She's home now.

> Go-karts could be fun
> If Evan and Q were here
> And, you know, engine

> Me, Evan, and Q
> Unstoppable warriors
> When I'm not grounded

> Sleepovers are the
> Best place for a friend like me
> I make them awesome

I peek across the front yard. Is Evan over at Q's yet? Are they already hanging out? Man, I wish I could be there. Before I was grounded, our sleepovers were legendary. Like, off the charts fun. On a scale of 1-10, they were a twelve for sure.

Without me there? His sleepover probably isn't

remotely fun. I'd say they're probably down to like, six-and-a-half, max. Definitely not maximum-level fun.

I mean, I'm trying, but I'm not having a lot of fun without them.

Chapter 4

It's Thursday, which is my favorite day. Thursdays are even better than Saturdays. And I get to sleep late on Saturdays. I like them so much that when Mom yelled at me to take out the trash, I didn't even yell back.

Thursdays are when Evan, Q, and I meet up at Mrs. Peddy's classroom after school for Science Club.

Mrs. Peddy is our club sponsor and the absolute best teacher ever. Why? Where do I start? Okay, for one, she's the only teacher I know who has a map of the solar system *and* a Minecraft poster in the same classroom. Another reason: Our class pet is an Emperor scorpion named Sugar.

The biggest reason of all, even bigger and cooler than a scorpion? Her never-ending supply cabinet. I know that sounds weird, but hear me out. I'm not talking about a shoebox full of popsicle sticks and pipe cleaners. I'm talking about a floor-to-ceiling cabinet chock full of extra batteries, marbles, paint, scrap wood, paper cups, soda cans... if you can build something with it, it's probably in there.

What makes Mrs. P the supreme coolest is that her

supply closet is off-limits to students—except for Science Club. It's awesome to have a teacher that doesn't treat us like we're little kids. I mean, we're practically middle schoolers already.

The way it works with Mrs. P is this: Let's say we want to make a potato-powered alarm clock. Potatoes aren't going to clock themselves, are they? We need supplies. How do we get supplies? We write a project proposal and submit it to Mrs. P. If she approves it, boom! She hands us keys to the closet.

Two weeks ago, Evan, Q, and I turned in our latest proposal. This project is going to be next-level amazing. With any luck, today we get to work.

I open the classroom door and take a deep breath. Ah, how I love the familiar aroma of Lysol and scientific greatness. It looks like Evan and Q are ready to go too. They're hunched over a paper, whispering. *Our paper*. Now that I'm here, I bet they'll want to get those supply closet keys and unleash the science.

Nicole Norris and her army of colored pencils and sketchbooks occupy the seat across from them. I drop my backpack in a chair and sit next to her. "Hey Nic."

She lowers her sketchbook long enough to say "hey" back.

I nod at my friends. "What's up? Is that our paper?"

Evan whispers to Q some more and hoists a "just a second" finger up, but Q looks across and smiles. He mutters something to Evan and slides the page in question across the table.

"Mrs. P gave us notes," Q says, right before his glasses tumble off the end of his nose.

I return them. "What'd she say?"

"Read it yourself, dorkus." Evan throws something small and solid at my face. A pink rubber eraser bounces off my forehead and lands in Nic's backpack. She fishes it out and hands it to me.

"Great shot, man," I say, because it was.

Q shoulder-checks him. "Chill."

Evan laughs.

I laugh, rub my forehead and retrieve our proposal page.

> Hypothesis: Does gaming relieve pain?
>
> 1) Ask two volunteers to sit in chairs.
>
> 2) Give volunteer number one a handheld video game to play. Give volunteer number two nothing.
>
> 3) Wrap hot towels around both volunteers' feet and start a stopwatch. Note how long it takes for each volunteer to yank their feet out from beneath the hot towels.

Mrs. P's swoopy red cursive nearly fills the margins. I've never seen so much red ink in one place before. My palms are spilling sweat, so I wipe them on my jeans and get reading.

This is what Mrs. Peddy wrote:

What an interesting hypothesis! I have questions for you:

1) What is your control in this experiment?
2) What are your variables?
3) Are you measuring all expressions of pain during the experiment or only the moment when the volunteers remove the towels?
4) Don't forget to consider internal processes. What is happening inside your volunteers during this experiment? It might help to draw a picture of how pain is being transmitted and received through the body, and how you think gaming might interrupt that transmission.
5) If we cannot provide heat, what other pain stimulus would work safely?

Keep working—you're almost there! Answer these questions and you'll get to use the supply closet.

Mrs. P

Huh. There's more left to do than I thought. Oh well. I like a hearty scientific challenge as much as the next guy. When Evan and Q and I put our heads together, we're pretty much unstoppable. There's nothing we can't accomplish if we put our minds to it, right?

"These questions aren't too tough, there's just a lot of them," I say. "We can get this knocked out in no time. The control is the volunteer without the videogame, right?"

Evan and Q flick a folded piece of notebook paper back and forth across the table.

"Guys?" No response.

Maybe they don't hear me. I say it again, louder this time. "Guys? If we get started now, we could get this done today."

Man, they are super into this paper triangle game.

"I think you're right. I already did the drawing part." Nic offers a color-coded sketch of pain traveling from the foot to the brain. It's a great sketch, but I'm confused. Why did she draw this?

"Wait. Did you join our group?"

Before she can answer, Evan pipes up. "We asked her to help." He scoots the paper triangle to Q then holds his thumb and forefingers together to make a target.

"Um, I asked you if you needed help," Nic corrects him.

"Whatever. That's okay, right Jeff?" Q asks.

Nic's nice enough, but this is Science Club. It's always been the three of us—me, Q, and Evan—in Science Club. They're acting like I ought to know what's going on. Did we talk about this before and I forgot? Or did they decide to do this and forget to ask me? Either way, there's no point arguing about it now.

"Yeah, sure." I scan Nic's drawing again. "This is really great, thanks." When I pass the sketchbook back, a loose page drops into my lap. It's a drawing of the three main characters from the original Fire Ant Heroes—Sergeant Sting, Queen Adlee, and the greatest warrior of them all, Tromma Tize.

"This is awesome! Did you draw this?" I hold the paper by the edges and hand it to her, careful not to smudge it.

Nic grins. "Do you like that? My friend Vince drew it for me in Art Club yesterday. You'd like him, he's a Fire Ant fanatic like you." Nic slides the fire ant drawing into a folder and picks up her sketchbook again. She points the end of her pen at different features of her pain sketch.

"Okay. Did you see this part? Here's where we introduce pain, at the foot. The peripheral nerve is here. That's what carries the pain signal through the spine to the brain."

"Where are you going to draw the, um, indoor—the endorphins?" I ask, trying to remember the name of the pain-reducing chemicals produced by the brain.

A giant snort from across the table derails my train of thought. "It sounded like you said *indoor phones*," Evan says. He and Q chuckle.

"Yeah, I guess." I shrug. "Whatever." I lock eyes with Nic and raise my eyebrows, like I'm saying *keep talking*.

"Maybe the endorphins go here?" She points to her sketch of the brain.

Evan and Q's chuckles snowball into loud laughter. Like, obnoxiously loud laughter. The kind that makes other kids look up from their projects and smile, like they want an invitation to the joke.

Ugh. Now Evan, because he's Evan, notices that he has the whole room's attention. What does he do? Well, he doesn't let that attention go to waste, that's for sure.

He catches his breath, then nudges Q and pulls his phone out of his back pocket. "Hello? Hello? Here, Jeff, it's for you—it's your indoor phone." Q snorts as Evan tries to pass his invisible phone to me.

"You're hilarious. Can we get to work now, please?"

"Ignore them." Nic continues sketching.

She's right. That supply cabinet isn't going to open itself. I scoop a pencil from my backpack, flip the proposal page over, and make notes on the back.

"I'll do the first question. Q, do you and Evan want to tackle the type of games we want to test?" Evan and Q huddle together, cackling. "Guys? Hey. Chuckles McGee. A little help?"

Just then, Mrs. Peddy walks over. "How are things going over here? There's a lot of noise from this corner of the room today."

Evan and Q go still and silent.

Mrs. Peddy peers over Nic's shoulder at her drawing and nods. "Great job, Nicole. Did you draw the cross-section of the spinal tract from memory?"

"No way. I Googled it." Nic holds her phone over her head to show Mrs. P where she found her resources. Mrs. P is big on resources.

"Excellent." One by one, she doles out her Teacher Look to each of us at the table. "Any questions for me, or are you all set?"

Under his breath, but loud enough that I can hear, Evan says "Yeah. Can Quenton and I work on something else instead?"

Q shakes his head and I swear he ever-so-slightly ooched his chair away from Evan. "We're all set, ma'am," Q says.

Mrs. Peddy moves on to the next table as I lean across ours and whisper-yell. "Dude. Is there a problem?"

Evan leans forward in his chair. "No problem. But hey, here's a hypothesis for you: Jeff Pennant won't come with us to GamerCon. Step one. Jeff asks his parents. Step two. Jeff's parents say no because he's grounded. Step three. There is no step three." His eyes lock onto mine and he leans back, crossing his arms like he's daring me to say something.

"Ha." I cross my arms back at him. "That's so not a hypothesis. A hypothesis has a definition of the problem, a proposed solution, and a predicted result. What you said was only a problem statement plus three steps. Two steps, actually."

"Whatever." Evan groans.

Nic sets her sketchbook aside and launches grenades at Evan with her eyeballs. "Not. Cool. Evan." She glares at him. I think she's trying to be nice to me, but it's not like I need her to defend me from my best friends.

"No, it's funny," I say. She makes a 'whatever' face. "It's funny because it's true, I do get grounded a lot." I put both hands on the edge of the table and face Evan and Q. "But not for GamerCon. No way. I'm grounded from electronics, yeah. But that doesn't include GamerCon."

"Sure. Okay." Evan shrugs and pulls out his phone like we're not having a conversation.

"It's not that big of a deal," Q jumps in. "But it's like, you always talk about your big ideas, all the cool stuff we should do. But man, you can't ever actually go do anything, ever. You get in trouble *a lot*. It's annoying, that's all."

He has no. Idea. How annoying this is. Seriously.

"We're supposed to be best friends, right?" Evan pokes his phone screen while he talks and doesn't look at me. "Best friends do stuff together. Besides school—and don't say Science Club or the bus because duh, those are school—when was the last time we all hung out?"

"Um, last week, when we made the bottle rockets."

"And you got grounded."

"Just for a week. It's over tomorrow."

"How about before that?"

"That's a great question, actually." Was it a month ago? No. The beginning of the school year? I don't know the answer. So I look at the ceiling. Maybe the answer will drop out of it into my brain. For the record, it doesn't. "I can't remember."

"That's because you're *always* grounded, dude, and you're always going to be grounded," Evan says. "It's almost like you try to get in trouble."

"That's so not true! Why would I *try* to get in trouble?

That's stupid. More importantly? That. Is. Not. True." Wait. *Am I raising my voice? I think I am.*

I glance around the room and everyone at Adam Ford's table has stopped working and is staring at me. Including Adam Ford who should totally mind his own business.

The bus monitor appears in the doorway. "Clear your areas and line up for the buses," Mrs. Peddy announces. Q and Evan bolt for the door. Nic mutters something about the girls' room and disappears into the slow-moving mob.

I shove our chairs under the table. This is not how I wanted Science Club to go.

When I get on the bus, Q's staring out the window. I'd sit next to him, but Alex Harris is already there, talking nonstop about Mothra. Neither of them looks at me when I walk past and sit in the empty row behind them.

I shouldn't let Evan and Q get under my skin, but they do. They're my best friends. It's not like they don't get in trouble with their parents either. But yeah, they're kind of right. Everything I say or do seems to make Mom and Dad mad. Whatever I ask them permission to do gets a big N-O. And then Evan and Q go hang out without me.

Again.

Chapter 5

Zip and his tennis ball greet me at the front door, which is reason number 47,872 why he is the best dog on the planet. He loves me whether I'm grounded or not. I scritch behind his ears, then he bolts for the back door. He knows what's next.

Outside, I chuck his worn-out ball toward the corner of the yard. Zip's so fast his black and white fur is a gray streak. He's ripping across the grass. Pretty soon, we've got a good rhythm going. My arms shift into autopilot. Throw—Race—Pick—Drop. Zip is a ball chasing machine. Then my brain plays and replays what Evan said at Science Club.

Best friends do stuff together.

The three of us have been best friends since first grade. We've been friends so long that our parents are friends.

It's almost like you try to get in trouble.

Well, no, Evan, I don't. Things go wrong sometimes. It's not my fault.

The sliding glass door scrapes open and snaps me out

of my thoughts. Mom hands me a juice box. "Hey. How was your day? Did you get to start your Science Club project?"

"No." I cringe a little at the edge in my voice.

"That's too bad. Wanna talk about it?"

I whip the ball in a different direction for Zip. "Meh." Explain my life to my mom? Where would I even start? Besides, I'd probably get in trouble for explaining it wrong.

"You seem upset, kiddo. Did you get a bad grade or something?"

"No, my grades are fine. I'm fine." *Factually accurate.*

"Is it friend stuff?"

I shrug.

"You know, tomorrow you're ungrounded. That's good news, right?"

Zip flops down at my feet and releases the ball. I pick it up and pluck leaf fragments off of the faded yellow fuzz. "Best news all week."

"Sadie's having friends sleep over tomorrow night. Would you like to invite Evan and Q to sleep over too?"

My heart pounds. Would I want to have my best friends sleep over? Is she messing with me? She'd better not be messing with me. I raise my "really?" eyebrows at her. "For real?"

"For real. You know your room has to be clean before anyone comes over."

"My room is fine."

"Do I need to check it myself?"

I squeeze the tennis ball so hard it might pop. "No

you do not. We agreed. Rooms are personal spaces unless there's an emergency. It's fine."

"I believe you. I need you to know—we cannot have a repeat of your last sleepover. We expect you to follow house rules. Do you understand?"

"I understand." Suddenly I'm smiling so hard it feels like happy lasers beaming from my face. "Thanks, Mom."

"Are you sure nothing's wrong?" She tussles my hair.

"Yeah. Nothing I can't handle." I want to jump up and down, but I'm in fifth grade so I have to act like it.

"That's the truth." She reaches down and scratches Zip's belly. "Your Dad and I are here, though, if you need help." She picks the empty juice box out of my hand and heads back inside.

"Come on, Zip!" We race inside, and down the hall to Sadie's room.

I knock and open the door at the same time. "Guess what?"

"You learned how to knock?"

"Ha. No. I mean, duh. But that's not it—Mom and Dad said I can have a sleepover tomorrow too!"

"Cool. What did you do to get ungrounded, exactly?"

"Um, I'm awesome, maybe? I don't know. I served my time and now it's done."

"Right. So. . . they gave you a second chance, huh? Or is it a third? I lose track."

I don't even care about her teasing, I'm so happy. "I'm—not—ground—ed!" I perform a small but powerful victory dance. It's spectacular. "Uh-huh. Ungrounded. That's right. You know it."

Finally. Things are starting to go my way. I dance out of Sadie's room, across the hall, and into my room. In my mind, Evan and Q are dancing right along with me.

Chapter 6

It's Friday afternoon. Evan and Q are going to be here any minute. What do you think my parents do?

"Jeff, we need to talk about the house rules. Have a seat." Mom pats the couch and Zip, who has been snoring under the coffee table, opens one eye. "We don't want a repeat of the last time you had people over."

Ugh. Fine. We reviewed The Rules twice last night before I could even call Evan and Q and tell them the good news. But whatever. I drop onto the couch next to Mom and sprawl out like a tired octopus. "I promise. No bottle rockets."

"That's a very good start. But remember—you are still grounded from screens. No phone. No video games."

Wait. What? "No video games?" I know I said I was fine with that, but I was hoping she wouldn't remember it. I sit up. "Come on, Mom. GamerCon's in two weeks. There are at least ten tournaments at GamerCon. We have to practice."

"You're lucky you still get to go to GamerCon," Mom

says.

"Dad! You guys can't be serious."

"Of course we can. We're the worst." Dad says. "Your mom already called Quenton's and Evan's moms to let them know not to bring electronics. Also—you should know—you and your friends are sleeping in the backyard."

Leave it to my parents to roll out new rules at the last minute. Inside my head, I shout *"Are you kidding me?"* but out loud, I manage to pull myself together and ask—mostly calmly—"What for? What's wrong with my room? Or the living room?"

Mom leans forward on the couch. "We're removing the temptation for you to get in more trouble. You can't play Xbox from the backyard. Plus, Sadie's having friends over too. Your Dad and I think it's better if both of you have privacy."

Dad spreads his arms wide. "You and your sister need your own personal space."

"So she gets the whole house to herself? You stick me in the backyard? How is that fair?"

"We're not 'sticking you in the backyard,'" Dad says. "You're camping out. There's a difference. Camping out is fun! Hey, remember the old telescope we used when we went on that trip to the mountains? I found it in the shed. If you clean the lens, you can watch the stars."

Stars. They're cool and all, but I haven't watched the stars since second grade. I groan.

Dad digs in. "I've already set up the tent and cots.

There's a lantern and a couple of flashlights on the patio for you. It might get a little chilly tonight, so wear warm pj's and take a few extra blankets on your way outside."

"It will be an adventure!" Mom waves her hands like pompoms.

"Calling something an 'adventure' doesn't magically make it awesome."

"Watch the attitude, kiddo. You realize how lucky you are to get to have a sleepover?" She looks me straight in the eyes. "These are your choices. You can take your sleepover to the backyard. Or you can cancel."

"Oh yay. It's an adventure." I say with all the enthusiasm of a broken robot. "Where are the extra blankets?"

"That's the spirit. Appreciate your childhood, my man. You're only a kid once." Dad claps me on the shoulder.

Chapter 7

Other than the pre-game lecture and the last-minute move to the backyard, I'm feeling mildly triumphant when Evan and Quenton show up. Still—I play it cool. Like Evan's meltdown yesterday in Science Club never happened. I mean, second chances and all, right?

Even better? Evan and Q aren't the least bit miffed about our banishment outdoors away from the Xbox. We haul our stuff out back and the evening is officially underway. We inspect our tent, and it's in great shape. No holes, rips, or mold anywhere. The worst thing about it is that we can hear Sadie and her friends' pop star singalong even from out here.

Evan and Q claim their cots then head straight for Dad's ancient telescope. Q plops on the ground and peers through the viewing scope. "Huh." He hops up and tilts the bearing box to get at the big meniscus lens at the other end. Evan darts around and examines the lens from behind Q's shoulder. They chatter like a couple of mechanics working on a broken-down car.

"Jeff, dude, you've got some kind of fungus on the inside," Evan says.

"I don't think it's fungus, actually." Q squints. "It looks like snail. . . or maybe slug trails."

"How would a slug get inside a sealed telescope?" Evan mops his forehead with his sleeve.

After some deliberation, we decide looking at the stars is out of the question. Too much slug and/or snail gunk.

Suddenly I remember the absolute most perfect thing we can do next. "Guys. We should build a go-kart. I've got a kit out in the garage."

"A go-kart?" Q peers down his glasses. "A model? Or an actual, full-size, legit go-kart?"

"Actual, legit."

"You think we can build a go-kart in one night?" Evan's left eyebrow lifts.

"We don't have to finish it tonight. Come on, I'll show it to you." I hop to my feet and motion for them to follow me. "It's out in the garage."

They don't move.

"You guys at least have to see it. It's pretty cool." I take a couple steps toward the kitchen door. "Come on, seriously."

"That's more of a 'you' project, dude," Evan says.

"Yeah, I think he's right. Go-karts take a long time to build." Q shrugs. "We need a short-term project."

"Okay, fine. I just thought it'd be fun." I open the shed door. "We can build something else. Maybe there's something in here we can use."

We begin our supply raid.

Evan finds some old fabric in a dusty cabinet. We loop one end of the cloth and tie it to the telescope tripod. Then we knot the other piece to the opposite side of the tripod, kind of like a handle.

"Gentlemen, we have ourselves a catapult," I announce. Q and Evan cheer.

That's more like it.

I point at our neighbor's house, about 30 yards beyond the back fence. "Whoever hits Mrs. Fischer's kitchen window gets a GamerCon t-shirt," I say. "Losers have to buy." Q and Evan look at each other then we race around the yard collecting pinecones.

We load the catapult, take aim, and fire. Pinecones pop-pop-pop against the wooden fence. Nobody comes close to hitting Mrs. Fischer's window. But we keep trying until we're out of both pinecones and daylight. It's no go-kart, but our catapult is capital-a Amazing.

"Well... I guess we're each buying our own shirts." Q sits on the patio and cleans his glasses with the corner of his sweatshirt.

"Anybody else hungry?" Evan asks.

"What time is it?" Q looks at his watch. "Woah. It's almost nine."

Who else has so much fun that they forget about food? Nobody. We are in awe of our own awesomeness. Evan and Q grab flashlights from the patio and rummage through the tent. Their supply report isn't promising. Nothing but blankets, bug spray, and hand sanitizer. We're not eating that.

As the host, it's my responsibility to sneak inside and loot the kitchen so my guests don't starve. The patio door is unlocked. I slide it open and stand like a statue for a moment, listening. Swoony, princess movie music floats out from the den. I give Evan and Q a thumbs-up through the glass door, then tiptoe to the fridge and the pantry. I stuff hot dogs, marshmallows, graham crackers, and chocolate bars down the front of my jacket, grab a bag of sandwich bread and am back outside without incident.

I triumphantly unload my jacket contents onto Q's cot and stand, arms open. I'm pretty sure I look as victorious and leader-like as I feel.

"Wait. Dude. Are those hotdogs raw?" Evan asks, squashing my balloon of pride.

"Well, I couldn't exactly microwave them and wake my parents."

"You know you can get worms from eating raw hotdogs, right?" Q blinks emphatically.

I seriously doubt that, but I shrug. "So we cook them."

Evan spreads his arms and twists side to side. "Do you see a stove?"

"Who needs a stove? Let's build a campfire," I say. Best idea ever, right?

"Bad idea, man," Q says.

"No. No way." Evan's eyes go huge.

"Come on. We don't want to get worms, do we? We gotta cook these."

"Why did you get food that needs cooking, anyway?" Evan asks. "Why didn't you grab chips or something? Go back in and get chips."

"We're camping, man. What's camping without hotdogs and s'mores?"

"Wait. You brought s'mores?" For a second, I think Q's on my side.

"No way. We can't build a fire in your backyard." Evan crosses his arms. Q crosses his too. It's two against one.

Let the record show that my friends are fun, but also they are giant babies.

I dig the fire pit all by myself.

I nab a lighter from the tool shed. Then I pile dry leaves in the bottom of the pit and ignite it. It takes, like, two minutes of feeding the fire like it's a hungry baby bird, dropping twigs and sticks into the pit one at a time. Then *fwoom*. Crackly flames stand tall. Smoke billows into the treetops. Neato.

I thread three hotdogs on a green stick and start cooking. Evan stands close by with the garden hose. Q has a bucket full of dirt. We're all ready for action.

"You know, I should keep this food for myself." I turn the stick slowly. "Since I'm doing all the work."

"You might be doing the work, but you're also the one who brought us raw food," Evan says.

"And, you know, you could have gone back inside

again. Picked something else. There's that," Q adds.

I ignore them, wrap each dog in a piece of bread and pull them off the stick. I take one and pass the rest to Evan, who takes one and passes the last dog to Q. I scarf mine down. It's perfect. Crispy on the outside, juicy on the inside.

While Evan and Q eat, I pull out the bag of marshmallows and get to toasting. That's when I hear the siren. Quiet at first, then louder. Then, louder with added lights. The three of us look at each other like, "Hey, fire truck."

We're still looking at each other when the whole mess screeches to a stop right in front of my house.

Then we're treated to the ear-splitting screams of four twelve-year-old girls as firefighters bust into the middle of their sleepover.

In that moment, Evan, Q, and I are immobilized. Well, Evan and Q are immobilized. I run for the safety of the tent.

Next thing I know there's a flashlight pointed at my face and a man's voice. "Out from behind the cot, now!" When there's a flashlight pointed at your face, you do what the shouting man says. I stand up, a little dizzy from the bright beam and the shouting. I follow the firefighter through the tent flaps just in time to see another firefighter spraying foam into my beautiful fire pit.

This is not what you want when you're camping.

A third firefighter dumps Evan's dirt bucket over the top. Like graham cracker sprinkles on a giant, smoky s'more.

A heavy, gloved hand flops onto my shoulder. "Where are your parents, son?" the firefighter with the flashlight asks. For a second, I forget how to talk.

I point to the window, where Mom, Dad, Mrs. Fischer, and two other firefighters are watching from inside. "There."

"Did you start this fire, or did your parents?" Captain Flashlight asks.

"I did, sir." I can't look at his face, so I examine the intricate stitching on my left shoe.

"I see. With your parents' permission?"

I shake my head. "They were asleep."

"So, that's a no, then." The giant man kneels in front of me, pivoting until I have no choice but to look at him. "You know, it's against the law to have an unattended fire pit."

I forget my embarrassment for a moment. We broke the law? Us? Criminals? No way.

"It wasn't unattended, though. *We* were attending it." I add "sir" at the end. "All three of us were." I point to Q and Evan, hiding behind a tree.

"I appreciate that, but you need *adults* to supervise, son," he says. "You're lucky your neighbor was watching out for you. This could have gotten out of hand fast." He holds his fist toward me, like he's asking for a fist bump, maybe. Before I can bump in return, he says, "Have a good night and stay safe," and tromps into the house.

This isn't the sleepover I wanted. This sleepover was supposed to impress my friends. It was supposed to prove to my parents I could be trusted to be un-grounded. To be free and have friends over. I followed the stupid rules they gave me. We stayed outside and didn't play video games or bother Sadie and her friends. But everything is still messed up.

I head across the yard to talk to Evan and Q. There's got to be a way we can salvage this night.

But before I can say a word, Q's mom barrels into the yard. Q lives across the street, so his mom probably freaked out when she heard the fire truck.

"Quenn-tonn, honey, are you okay?" She pulls him into an overpowering hug, then snakes an arm around Evan and draws him in close. "Evan, I've called your mom, she wants me to bring you home." He nods.

"Hi, Mrs. Maxwell. Sorry about the sirens."

She peers over her glasses and locks eyes with me. "I am too, Jeffrey." She marches toward the back door, a kid under each arm. Evan and Q don't say a word.

I trail them like I'm pulled by a magnet. I get that Q's mom is taking him home, but come on, does she have to take Evan too?

Mrs. Maxwell doesn't slow down once she reaches the kitchen. I do, though. Because I spot Mrs. Fischer, my parents, and The Firefighter-With-The-Flashlight at our dinner table. The deep wrinkles in Mom's forehead tell me they're having a serious conversation.

As much as I want to get Evan to stay—or even tag along over to Q's—I *really* don't want Mom and Dad to see me. So I back out of the room, onto the patio, and gently close the sliding door.

My legs feel like cement blocks and my eyes itch. I drag myself to the lonely tent, wrap myself in a smoky blanket and stretch out on my cot.

All that's left for me to do is lay here and wait for the inevitable doom that is my parents.

Chapter 8

Maybe I dozed off. By the time I hear the fire truck rumble down the street, it feels like ages have passed. Then I feel a cool hand on my face.

"Are you okay?" Mom brushes the hair off my forehead, leans over, and plants a kiss on top of my head.

"Yeah," I roll onto my side. Experience tells me that this "are you okay" question paired with a kiss does not necessarily mean that doom is not forthcoming. I wait.

"Good," Mom steps back and holds the tent flap open. "I'm glad you're not hurt. But son, you have a lot of explaining to do."

There it is. Train to Doomville, approaching the tracks. Stand clear of the doors.

"Yes ma'am." I sit up and shove my hands into my sweatshirt pockets.

Dad ducks into the tent and sits on the cot where Q's sleeping bag used to be. He clasps his hands together, leans forward, and looks me in the eyes. "You scared your mother and me to death! What were you thinking?" His voice is stern but he's not yelling.

"I was thinking a few things. We were hungry, that's one thought. Also, I thought about how you don't like it when I use the microwave and make noise in the kitchen late at night." *Factually accurate.*

"Building a fire is not the answer to that problem, son. We live in a neighborhood. You could have done a lot of damage." He rubs his forehead with the palm of his hand.

"But I didn't set fire to the whole neighborhood, did I? I was safe! I dug a pit, just like the ones we use when we camp."

"If Mrs. Fischer hadn't looked out her window, who knows what might have happened?" Mom asks. Her voice is knotted like the end of a balloon, tight and squeaky.

Is she kidding? I know exactly what would have happened. "Well, I would have made s'mores, for one thing. When we were done, Evan would have dumped sand on the fire, and Q would have poured water on top of that. Then we probably would have talked about GamerCon and gone to sleep. We would have had a blast, actually. It would have been great. I had it all covered. You never trust me. Why don't you trust me?" I'm sweaty now.

"We don't trust you because you make these kinds of choices," Mom says.

"You could have set the house on fire. How do you not understand that?" Dad asks through both his hands, which are now covering his entire face.

"Well, yeah, guess I *could* have, but I wouldn't have. I

didn't."

Dad says something that sounds like a whole bunch of vowels strung together.

"You need to understand that your actions have consequences." Mom's hands are on her hips. If she glared any harder at me her eyes would be closed.

"I *know*. I'm surrounded by consequences," I flop sideways on my cot. "We stayed outside. We didn't use our phones or play video games. I followed the rules. I can't help it if Mrs. Fischer's nosy."

"You think *Mrs. Fischer* is the problem here?" Mom accelerates into full-on yelling. "Mrs. Fischer is not the problem! You owe Mrs. Fischer an apology for scaring her half to death!"

"I don't owe Mrs. Fischer anything! She owes *me* an apology for ruining my night! Now things are going to be even worse with Evan and Q, and it's all her fault. No—It's her fault and *your* fault for your stupid rules. This wouldn't have happened if we could have just stayed inside and played Fire Ant Heroes like we'd wanted."

The tent is silent except for the sound of Mom inhaling. Then exhaling.

"Well, you'd better get used to it. Until you learn how to accept responsibility and use some common sense, there will be no phones, no games, no friends over, and no GamerCon."

She says it casually. Like she didn't just end my best friendships.

I bolt upright. "What do you mean, 'no GamerCon?'"

"I mean exactly what I said. You're not going to GamerCon." She opens the tent flap and Dad stands.

"But Mom! You can't do that! Dad, tell her she can't do that!" Hot tears fill my eyes.

"You should have thought about that before you built the fire, son." He's no help at all.

Mom motions to me like she wants me to get up, but I don't budge. "It's late. We're all too tired for this conversation. Come inside and go to bed. We'll talk more in the morning."

Dad hunches his way out of the tent. "Jeffrey. Let's go."

I grab my lantern and follow them. By the time I get to the kitchen, they're already down the hall. "We're not talking in the morning!" I shout at their bedroom door. "I'm not talking to you ever again!"

"Go to bed! Get some sleep!" Dad's voice sails down the hall.

I stomp back to my room, climb into bed, and wrap myself like a burrito in the covers.

I wish I could have shown Mom and Dad my fire pit and told them what big chickens Evan and Q had been about cooking the hotdogs. I want them to be impressed by my self-sufficiency. I want them to be proud of my creative problem-solving. But it's obvious that they aren't.

Right now, I'm the campfire, Mom and Dad are the firefighters, and I'm soaked in "we're disappointed in you" foam.

I'm breathing ragged, feeling like I just ran the mile in gym class. Go to sleep? How in the world am I supposed to *sleep*? Mom's voice saying "no GamerCon" bounces between my ears.

This is officially the new worst sleepover of my entire life.

Chapter 9

The sun doesn't care how mad I am. It rises anyway.

Even though I'm lying in bed, I feel like I hit a wall. With my face. A huge, concrete, immovable wall named Matt and Mallory Pennant.

My parents.

"Appreciate childhood because you're only a kid once," they say.

"Enjoy eleven, Jeff, because things are different when you're grown up," they say.

Okay, I say, *yes*. I will. I will enjoy my childhood. I will live life to the fullest.

Then what happens?

Are they proud of me for doing exactly what they told me to do? The answer is no. It's a big, fat, hairy, capital-N nope. They aren't proud. They're the exact opposite.

Ugh. I flop onto my belly and smush my forehead into the cool pillow. Why are they doing this to me? In what world do they think keeping me from GamerCon with Evan and Q is a good idea? How can they not know how important it is? I can't—repeat, CAN NOT—miss this.

My friendships are on the line.

My bedroom door squeaks and I smell bacon at the same time.

"You hungry? Dad made breakfast lasagna." Sadie's the only other person in the family allowed in my room. We kind of have an understanding. She doesn't mess with my stuff, and I don't sneak into her room and play Plushie Armageddon with her stuff while she's at dance class. Usually.

She sits on the edge of my bed, carefully holding a plate piled high with layers of fluffy pancake, syrup, bacon, and sliced strawberries. It looks and smells amazing, but I'm too blergh to eat.

"No." I yank my Tromma Tize fleece blanket over my head.

"Okay then, more for me." Sadie sets the plate on my bedside table and gently peels Tromma off of my head and shoulders. "Come on, dude. What's going on?"

"Don't you have friends over or something? Go bug them." I thrash onto my side facing away from her, grab a corner of the blanket and tuck it under my arm.

She scoots close enough that I can smell bacon on her breath. "They all left after, you know, the firefighters showed up. Um, about that? What happened?"

"I don't want to talk about it."

"You don't want to talk about what? Setting fire to the yard, or missing GamerCon? Yeah. I heard."

Why won't she go away? Maybe if I lay here in silence, she'll get the hint.

I wait.

She doesn't move.

Well played, my persistent sister.

"Fine. I don't know what you want me to say. If I don't get to hang out with Evan and Q, I'm pretty much friendless. That's what they've done. They've grounded me from ever having friends again."

"Did Mom and Dad say that? That you're grounded from having friends? That's a weird thing to ground somebody from."

I flip over to face her. "No, that's not *exactly* what they said. But that's what's going to happen."

"Are you sure?"

"Of course I'm sure. I'm one hundred percent sure."

"How do you know?"

My face is hot, and I don't think it's because of the blanket. "If I can't hang out with Evan and Q because I'm grounded all the time, then, you know, they move on. They hang out without me. Mom and Dad are always grounding me for something. Even when I do exactly what they say, I end up in trouble. It's so not fair. It's like they don't want me to have friends."

"That stinks. But I don't think that's really what Mom and Dad want, do you?"

I push myself upright and lean against the wall. "Who knows what they want? I mean, it was Mom's idea for me to have a sleepover. Her idea. Not mine. I didn't mind, but I didn't ask for it. And then, *then*—they give me all these rules to follow—I mean, we had to sleep outside, we couldn't game. It was ridiculous. But I did everything they said to do. You'd think they'd be happy. Right? Nope. I still get grounded."

Sadie nods and offers the plate of break-sagna again. This time I take the plate and pick a piece of bacon out of the warm, sticky center.

"I don't get why parenting seems so hard for them. It's not like they couldn't have known what to expect. I didn't randomly appear one day, like—SURPRISE! You have a son! They had plenty of time to prepare."

Sadie giggles. "And it's not like there aren't parenting books."

"Right? Ever get lost in a bookstore? I have. The first place I look for Mom or Dad is the parenting section. They're almost always there." I chomp half a slice of bacon in one bite.

"I think they might own enough parenting books to open their own library."

"Have you ever looked at those books?" I ask. "The titles are kind of insulting when you think about them. "What to Do When You Don't Know What to Do with Your Kid Anymore?"

"Did you see the one Dad's reading right now?" Sadie asks. "'Fifteen Steps to Getting Your Life Back from Your Children.' It's a classic."

"Oh, come on. Really? That's what he's reading?"

Sadie nods.

"How many books are there for kids about how to handle their parents?"

"I don't know."

"None. I mean, I've never seen one, have you?"

Sadie shakes her head.

"Why not? Why don't kids get any help? How are we supposed to figure out the tough stuff? Like, for example, why they say things like 'have fun, be a kid,' and then WHAM take everything away from us because we had fun?"

"Nobody else can figure it out either, I guess. Otherwise, there would be a book about it. Or at least a *haiku*." Sadie pinches my big toe.

Maybe it's the bacon and berries, maybe it's my sister's pinch, but I feel better. Like I'm looking at a blurry screen, then—snap—it's sharper, brighter. I know she was teasing me, but Sadie gave me an idea.

And it's brilliant.

"That's it! I know what to do." I scramble out from under the blanket and off the side of the bed.

"You're writing a *haiku* about Mom and Dad, aren't you?"

"Better than a haiku." I rifle through the stack of books on my bookshelf until I find a well-loved copy of *The Backyard Guide to American Birds, Vol. 12*, and pass it to my sister.

"Birds? Your brilliant idea is birds?" Sadie blinks.

"Not exactly. A book. A field guide to parents. Remember that obnoxious bird that used to nest right outside? It drove me nuts, chirping all the time, crashing into my window, right? I didn't get what it was doing. So Dad gave me this book." I tap the cover. "I looked up the bird, read about it. Figured out I needed to close my curtains so the window wouldn't confuse it as much."

"But. . . birds?" She flips through the glossy pages.

"Not birds. Parents. I don't get our parents. Why do they ground me when I follow the rules? They're going to cost me my best friends if I don't do something about it."

"So you're getting them birds."

"No, pay attention. I'm going to research and write myself a guidebook like this one. See? It's perfect! I'll learn everything I can about Mom and Dad. I'll figure out what makes them happy, then I can do those things. If they're happy, they'll unground me and I can get my life back."

Sadie's nose wrinkles as she squints at me. "That's not a terrible idea, but why write a whole book about it?"

"So many reasons. One, if "Fifteen Steps to Getting Your Life Back from Your Children" is a best-seller, my book's got a chance. Two, Mrs. P makes us take notes because she says we remember what we write. When I find something that makes Mom and Dad less mad, I want to remember it. And three—I just want to, okay? You could help me if you want."

"I might. Maybe."

"You have to admit, it's genius."

"I wouldn't call it genius. Clever, maybe." She stands, picks up my empty plate and fork, and makes her way to the door. "Glad you're okay."

I'm not only okay, I'm on fire.

Look, I know I'm not the only kid in the world who's ever been grounded. I'm not stupid. But I've lost everything good because the grown people in my life don't make any sense. I know I'm not a parent. But I'm pretty sure doing what you say you'll do is in the top five rules of parenting. It's right up there with feed the kid.

Just my opinion.

If I can figure out how to make them happy, I can hang out with Evan and Q. The three of us can go to GamerCon and we'll get our friendship back on track.

I dig out my notebook and pen, sit at my desk, and prepare to write the book that will change my life.

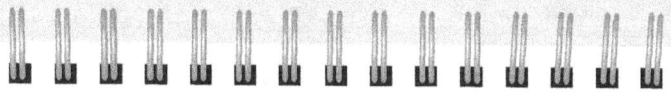

HOW TO RAISE HAPPY PARENTS
by JEFF PENNANT

CHAPTER ONE

This book will examine the natural mystery of the American parent. We'll look at who and what parents are, understand their basic features, and try to answer the question: What makes parents happy?

In my eleven years on this earth, I've spent a lot of time in my room. I've missed out on sleepovers, lost screen time and phone privileges, and am very likely going to lose my best friends.

Why? Because of my parents.

So let's begin.

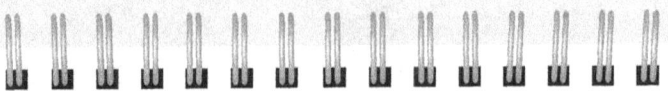

WHO AND WHAT ARE PARENTS:

Parents are the two main people on the planet who are supposed to love you, teach you, and basically guide you into adulthood. If anyone's going to show you the ropes about life, it's your parents. They're your family.

My grammy always said when God decided to reveal Himself on earth, He could have shown up on a spaceship, or as a tree, or riding a pterodactyl, but He didn't. What did He pick? He chose to be born into a family. An ordinary family with a regular Mom and Dad. So that tells us that families are important. Maybe even the most important, since that's where He started His visit.

Families can be one parent, or even grandparents, aunts and uncles, or foster parents. For purposes of this research, I will use my parents as the examples, with the understanding that your parents may vary.

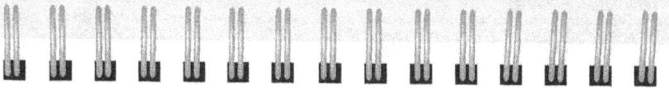

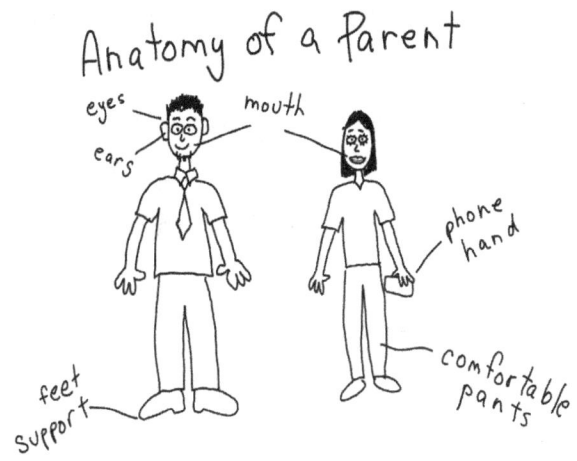

Anatomy of a Parent

Eyes: Moms and Dads sometimes have sensitive eyes. For example, my parents' eyes are easily overwhelmed by the sight of dust, dirt, fire, and original wall paintings. When I was little, my mom tried to tell me she had eyes in the back of her head. I discovered—and she confessed—that this is false.

Ears: My parents prefer the absence of sound while at home. Or limited, muted sound. I know this because I receive daily requests to "Turn that off, please. I need quiet." Some parents like listening to music, or podcasts, or the news. Mine do not.

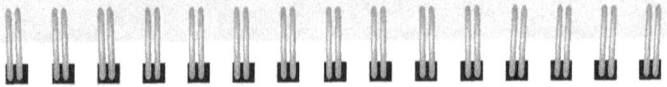

Mouth: Coffee and food go here. Most importantly, and obviously, the mouth is also where talking and yelling come from.

Phone Hand: They check their phones at regular intervals and complain often about other people's lack of "interpersonal skills." They prefer my phone hand to be empty.

Comfortable Pants: This is what my parents put on as soon as they get home from work. They wear these exclusively on evenings and weekends (except to church or out to dinner).

Foot/Ankle Support: Due to the mobile nature of parenting, Mom and Dad almost always wear footwear that allows them to walk and/or run.

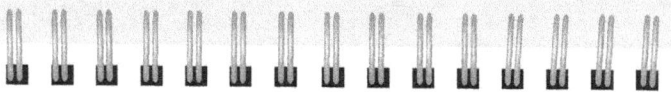

ESSENTIAL FEATURES:

Eating: Parents eat a minimum of three meals daily, snacks not included.

Sleeping: They never get enough of this.

Energy: Varies, depends on Eating and Sleeping

Work: Dad is an accountant at the community college bookstore. Mom is a marketing assistant at a real estate agency. I don't know exactly what either of those things are, but I know some days they like their jobs and some days they don't.

Chores: They clean, cook, and do laundry, in no particular order.

Hobbies: They tell my sister and me to clean, cook, and do laundry, also in no particular order and without any warning. That seems to amuse them.

They sometimes watch TV, usually boring things like nature documentaries or home improvement shows. Mom and Dad like movies, but they argue about what kind to watch, so Sadie or I usually get to pick. Then they fall asleep and snore through the whole thing, but when they wake up, they're happy (see "Sleeping").

PROBLEM STATEMENT:

My parents are always unhappy with me. They're so unhappy with me that they never let me do anything, have anything, or go anywhere. To prove I'm not exaggerating, here's a partial list of all the things I've been denied over the past few months:

WHAT I ASKED FOR:	WHAT THEY SAID:
Wheelie shoes	Not appropriate for school—Dad
Summer wheelie shoes	You'll break your arm—Mom
Hoverboard	Waste of money—Mom and Dad
Virtual reality goggles	You already have real reality—Dad
Mini drone	Too small, you'll lose it—Mom
Regular drone	You have plenty of toys—Dad
My own computer or tv	Absolutely not, it rots your brain—Mom
More screen time	First chores, then screens—Mom and Dad
New phone	(See screen time)

WHERE I ASKED TO GO:	WHAT THEY SAID:
Space station camp	Houston is entirely too far to travel on a school night. —Mom
Adventure safari	Who needs to go to Africa when you have a perfectly good imagination? —Mom
Northspire Mall Food Court	hahahahahahahahaaaa *breaths* hahahahahahahahaaa —Dad
GamerCon	Was yes, but now no —Mom and Dad

PRACTICAL APPLICATIONS: THE VISUAL GUIDE TO PARENTAL HAPPINESS

How can we tell whether Parents are happy? Charts are excellent guidance tools. Having trouble seeing across the classroom? Go to the eye doctor—you'll read a chart. Want to know how to identify poisonous snakes? Somebody's made a chart. Want to better understand your parents? Please, friend, help yourself to this chart.

I like to call this the Visual Guide to Parental Happiness. Refer to this guide for help recognizing the varying signs and degrees of happiness in your parent.

Visual Guide To Parental Happiness

(angry face)	Guaranteed Grounding
(shocked angry face)	Steer Clear
(stern face)	Proceed With Extreme Caution
(slight smile face)	Somewhat Happy
(big smile face)	Full Happy

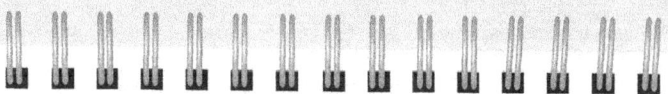

What you see in this picture is the stage known as Guaranteed Grounding: You don't want your parents to

make this face. Trust me, I know. I've seen it a lot. Notice the puffed-out cheeks. Guaranteed Grounding cheeks look like they have a lot of yelling stashed inside. There are a lot of angry words in there, and when you see this face, you know that all those words are about to come out.

Also worth noting—their eyebrows. Guaranteed Grounding eyebrows look like furious scorpions.

As you can see, at this stage, there's not a hint of a smile. Your parents' lips are pressed together so hard they are barely visible. Some parents' lips may even blend seamlessly with bright red, angry cheeks.

When my parents are this mad, I sometimes wonder what will happen if I look directly into their eyes. Will I turn to stone? Do they have lasers? I know sometimes people have a hard time looking directly into someone else's eyes.

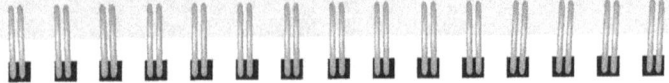

That's cool. And when laser eyes have been developed, also probably safer.

Guaranteed Grounding is amazing to see in person. And slightly terrifying, like when you see great white shark feeding time at the aquarium.

If Guaranteed Grounding is a pot of water boiling over, Steer Clear is a constant simmer. At this level, parents are not mad enough to assign a punishment. But they are mad enough that instead of speaking like a normal human, their mouths splutter a bunch of vowel sounds. Like Guaranteed Grounding, we can easily identify Steer Clear by the eyebrows: I call these "mountain climbing caterpillars of doom."

Another telltale sign of Steer Clear is the jaw. If your parents' jaws drop like this, you are definitely in Steer Clear territory. Whatever you're doing when you see this, stop

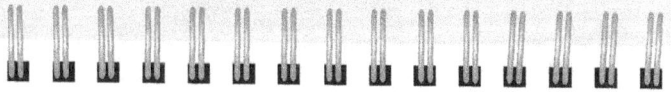

doing it. Back away slowly. Wait quietly. *

*I've never actually attempted to do this with my parents. I have witnessed my friend Q successfully use this method with our neighbor's angry dog, though. It seems like it would work with parents.

The level beneath Steer Clear is Proceed With Extreme Caution. Proceed With Extreme Caution is the clackety whir of a rattlesnake's tail. It's a warning. What does this warning look like? It looks like my parents' faces when I ask to use the power drill: blank, emotionless mystery. I don't know what this face is about to do. Are my parents mad? Are they about to fall over laughing?

I. Don't. Know.

I'm prepared for anything just in case.

Once in a while, my parents start a day in Somewhat Happy. This level is what happens when your parent wakes up in a good mood but then they open the electric bill. Or a note from your gym coach. Depending on Mom and Dad's recovery time, a Somewhat Happy day is not a bad day. But it's not award-winning. You can easily spot Somewhat Happy by the mostly relaxed, sort-of-smiling expression, and by the use of complete words and sentences.

Finally, we reach the dream level. The Full Happy. This level is what we all hope for in life. At my house, this level exists only in my memory.

If I compare my parents' faces to the Visual Guide, it's obvious: My parents spend most of their time bouncing between the Steer Clear and Guaranteed Grounding stages.

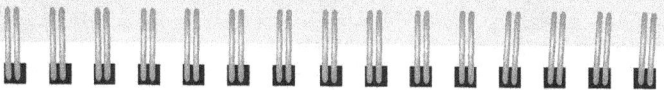

Maybe that's why I can't ever do anything fun and am about to lose my best friends.

Maybe if my parents spend more time in Full Happy mode, I spend less time grounded and get to live my best life.

It's a theory.

So here are my questions and problems to solve:

1) Why do parents get angry?
2) What can kids do to make them happy?
3) How fast can a kid switch his parents from Guaranteed Grounding to Full Happy?
4) What will it take to do that?

Chapter 11

Guess who was so excited about writing a book so he can get ungrounded that he completely forgot about today's spelling test but still scored 90 out of 100? That's right. This guy.

After the test, we head to the library for independent reading time. The latest Fire Ant Heroes graphic novel sits in its spot on the shelf. *Score!* I nab it and settle in to read.

Then an odd, hissing-coughing sound catches my attention. It's Mrs. Peddy, whispering "Jeff. Jeff," from across the room.

"Hey Mrs. P.," I whisper back, and I wave. She flaps her hands until I realize she's motioning me to join her. I sling my backpack over my shoulder and head to the library doorway.

Teachers never talk to me outside of class. Am I in trouble? Did I forget to turn in a permission slip? What could this be about? *Oh, great.* Now my palms are sweaty. Sweat and graphic novels don't mix.

Mrs. P. smiles and leans forward, speaking quietly.

"How are you today, Jeff?"

"Good, thanks. Did I forget an assignment or something?"

She shakes her head. "You? No, of course not. I'm sorry to interrupt your library time, but I'm on my way to an appointment and noticed your class was here. I was hoping to speak with you. Could I ask you a personal question?"

"Okay. I mean, I guess it depends on what you're asking about."

"In Science Club last week, right before the buses arrived, your table was louder than usual. To be more specific, *you* were a little louder than usual." her voice is gentle, like a grandma's, but her expression is serious. "You left before I could ask you about it. I was concerned. Is everything okay?"

My face feels over-inflated, like a tire. And hot. I have a hot, over-inflated tire for a face. Mrs. Peddy will probably notice that, too. Apparently, she sees and hears everything.

I take a deep breath. "It's not a big deal. We were just messing around." It's true. At least, it was true until the moment we weren't messing around anymore.

Mrs. P studies my face for a second, and I wonder if she believes me. "Hmm. Well, you know your friends better than I do, but the tone of your conversation didn't sound like you were 'messing around' in a very fun way. But—" She pauses, her features relax, and she smiles— "I'm glad I was mistaken. If you ever need to talk, my door is open. I wanted to let you know that. Okay?"

"Yeah. It's okay, thanks, Mrs. P." I say. I try to laugh casually, like *what a funny idea that you just had that was silly and wrong,* but it comes out sounding like a nervous chipmunk.

"What are you reading?" She motions toward the graphic novel in my hand.

I show her the cover. "Fire Ant Heroes," she reads. "What beautiful art. That looks like a fun read. You read a lot of different types of books, don't you?"

My favorite teacher showed up in the library to ask if I'm okay. And she thinks FAH art is beautiful. How do I describe this feeling? It's like finding a hidden stash of armor tucked under a shrub in FAH3. It's a bonus resource type of happy.

"Yeah. You know what else? I write books too." I pull my notebook out of my backpack and flip to chapter one. "It's kind of a scientific project."

"A scientific project? I'm intrigued." She raises her eyebrows and looks at me approvingly.

I nod as I pass the notebook to her. Mrs. Peddy accepts it with both hands like it was an award, and I feel like I've won a prize too. As weird as this might sound, I can't help but want to impress her. I chew on my lip as she reads so I don't accidentally victory dance.

"You have an interesting way with words, Jeff," she says. *Is that a good thing or a bad thing, I wonder?* "I like your list of questions and problems to solve. Do you think you could approach this problem like one of your Science Club project proposals?"

When she says Science Club, I get a little jab in my chest. Evan, Q, and I used to rule Science Club together. Now? Not so sure. If I do this right, we will again. "You mean, like write this in Science Club?"

"No, not exactly. I mean develop a strong hypothesis, create experiments, establish a control group."

"With my parents? How do I do that?"

Mrs. P smiles. "It's not my place to tell another scientist how to run their experiment or write their book. But as your teacher, I'll ask you this: What is a scientist's most important tool?"

That's easy. "Observation skills."

"Correct." she flips through the pages. "You've already made some good observations about your mom and dad's *appearance*. Maybe observing your parents' *behavior* will help you develop a testable hypothesis. What people *do* is a far more important clue about who they are than what they *say*." She hands the notebook back to me. "I really do need to get going. Thank you for sharing that with me. Keep me posted on your progress? I'll see you in class."

I drop back into my reading spot, but I can't concentrate on Fire Ant Heroes. I hadn't planned to show my Field Guide to anyone—at least, not at first. But Mrs. P knows her science, and her suggestions in Science Club always make our projects cooler. So if I'm going to share it with anyone, Mrs. P is at the top of the list. And if she says I should observe behavior, that's what I'll do.

I mean, I know it's not going to be easy, but I feel like my chances to get ungrounded in two weeks are pretty good. I've got a plan, sort of. I've got Mrs. P and science in my corner. And come on, I almost aced that spelling test without even trying.

This will work. I can feel it.

Because let's face it: I'm carrying the hopes and dreams of every kid who's ever been grounded. If I do this right, not only will I get my best friends back, one day, there will be awards. I may even have my own YouTube channel.

I'll go ahead and say this now: You're welcome world.

The bell rings and I strut to the cafeteria like the best-selling self-help author I'm going to be someday.

Chapter 12

"Hey. How'd you do on the spelling test?" I walk around to the seat next to Evan and sit. They both nod, but neither of them says anything. All of fifth grade has spelling tests on the same day, so I know they know what I'm talking about. I repeat. "You guys. How'd you do on the spelling test?"

"Eighty." Evan stares at his lunch tray. "I studied last night for an hour."

"Cool, cool." I unroll my lunch bag. "How about you, Q-man?"

"I got an 85."

"There were only ten words. Ten points each. How'd you get 85?" I pull the crust off my sandwich.

"Mr. Nguyen gives us a bonus word," Q says.

I sip my milk and stare at Q, then at Evan. This is the spot in the conversation where they're supposed to ask me what I scored. But they don't. "Cool. Yeah. I forgot about the test. Like, completely."

Q raises his chin and blinks at me through smudgy

glasses. "Oh, no."

"Oh, yeah." I unwrap my peanut butter and jelly then pause for dramatic effect. "I got a 90 though."

"You cheated, didn't you," Evan said. It wasn't even a question.

"Jeff, that's not cool." Q scorn-wrinkles his forehead.

"I didn't cheat! That's my score for real." Grape jelly blops from my sandwich onto the lunch table.

"No way you only missed one word." Evan leans so close to his tray he's almost wearing his lunch.

"Yes way."

"What word did you miss?"

I hang my head in pretend shame. "Congruent."

"I missed that one too." Q picks a stray kernel of corn from his lasagna and returns it to the corn compartment on his sectioned lunch tray.

"Yeah. That one is tough," I say. We have a moment of silence for challenging spelling words.

"Q. You still coming to soccer practice tonight?" Evan gathers his napkin and utensils on his tray and stands. He's acting like I'm not even here.

Soccer?

"What time?" Q rises from his seat.

Wait a minute. Are we leaving?

"5:30. My mom said we could give you a ride home after." Evan waits for Q to join him and they slowly walk toward the garbage bins.

"Soccer practice? What soccer practice? When did we

start playing soccer?"

Have I stumbled into some kind of alternate universe? What is going on?

I scramble to my feet and head toward the cafeteria doors. But then the lunchroom monitor blows his whistle. "Pick up your trash, Pennant!"

I spin around and race-walk back to the table as fast as I can. I grab my milk bottle in one hand and lunch bag in the other and hustle toward the trash bin. About halfway there, though, my traitor of a right foot slides out from beneath me. I mean it flies straight up like gravity is less of a law and more of a nice idea. Next thing I know, I'm horizontal in the air, staring at the tiled ceiling for a fat two seconds. Then cold, sticky floor greets my back.

WHAM.

I'm flat on my back in a pile of somebody else's lasagna, right in front of Trevor Wickham and his friends. Air returns to my lungs and I wait for Trevor to say something snarky, but he doesn't. He and his friends keep talking.

I listen to the buzzing noise bouncing between my ears. After another breath, I recognize the sound. It's laughter. I lift my head—ouch—and see Evan and Q doubled over, laughing so hard they're red-faced and sweaty.

Double ouch.

I roll onto my side and spot a familiar pair of purple glitter leggings. "Shut *up*, you jerks! Jeff, are you okay?" Nicole kneels next to me and yells over her shoulder. "Vince! Bring paper towels?"

I know she means well, but ugh. The last thing I want at this moment is more attention.

I push myself to my feet and feel the room shrink and spin at the same time. "I'm fine, thanks."

Evan and Q wipe laugh-tears from their eyes and wander out of the cafeteria. I want to follow them, but I can't. Something's pinning my shoes to the floor.

"Hang on." That something is Nic. She extracts lasagna noodles from my shoelaces, stands next to me, and holds my arm like I'm her grandpa. "Ignore them, they're being toads."

"Sure you're all right, man? You don't look good." Vince hands me a wadded-up ball of paper towels and I wipe sauce off the back of my jeans.

I might like Vince's drawing skills, but I don't need his sympathy. "I said I'm fine, didn't I? I have to go." I need an explanation from Evan and Q. And I need out of the cafeteria. I leave Nic holding the noodles and head for the double doors, but Mr. Paul, the lunchroom monitor, intercepts me before I can get there.

"Sorry sir, after a fall like that, you're not going anywhere but to Nurse Traci's office," says Mr. Paul. Next thing I know he leads me out of the cafeteria, down the administration hallway, and into the nurse's office.

I've never been to Nurse Traci's before. She smells like strawberry hand sanitizer when she's sitting across from me. Up close, though, she smells like she's eaten a whole bag of sour cream and onion potato chips. Unfortunately, she checks my eyes and head. So there's a lot of sour cream and onion in my afternoon.

She hands me a package of wet wipes and helps me wring tomato sauce and cheese from my hair. I don't say much, but I don't have to. She does all the talking. She asks me if I feel nauseous and I tell her no. She asks me if anything hurts. I tell her nothing hurts. Which is true, unless you count the sore spot on the back of my head and the stinging shame of embarrassment. Oh, and being laughed at by your best friends. That does hurt. It hurts quite a bit, in fact, but I don't tell her about that part.

By the time Nurse Traci hands me an "I'm All Better" slip recess is over, so I slide into Mrs. Peddy's classroom in time for Social Studies. Usually, I hate missing recess. If recess was anything like lunch today, though, it's a good thing I missed it.

Since when do Evan and Q play soccer? Why wouldn't they tell me about it? I don't know what their problem is, but I know for sure they have one.

With me.

Chapter 13

I sit by myself at the front of the bus, ready for the ride home. Nic sits by herself across the aisle from me. She's reading a graphic novel I've been wanting to check out from the library.

Ordinarily, I might ask her about it, but a) she'll act like we're BFFs even though we're so not and b) the headache pounding in my skull says, 'No Talking Please'. Instead, I stare out the window and wonder why Q isn't on the bus yet but then I remember. Today he and Evan are playing soccer.

Steve McCrory holds his nose as he walks past me and yells "Hey, adybody else sbell la-zad-ya?"

I stand up behind him in the aisle, hold my arms wide, and take a giant bow. My head hurts so bad, it feels like my brains are about to topple out of my ears, but at least everybody on the bus cracks up. I return, victorious, to my seat.

Har har, Steve.

But yeah. I do smell lasagna. As soon as I get to my

house, I ditch my t-shirt and jeans in the entryway and flop face-first on the couch. Zip sticks his snout into the pile of clothes, sneezes, and backs away. Even my dog thinks my clothes smell weird. *Ugh.*

I'm supposed to go straight to my room after school, but I'm exhausted. I'll lie here for one minute then grab my clothes and go. One tiny minute, that's all. I let my eyelids drop and start counting to sixty just to be safe.

One. Was it just this morning that I was feeling good about my chances of going to GamerCon with Evan and Q? My day rocketed from A-plus to F-minus in seven hours. That's got to be some kind of record.

Two. What is the deal with Evan and Q? I thought they didn't like soccer. Why didn't they tell me they were signing up? Maybe they didn't ask me to sign up with them because I'm grounded. I mean, why would they bother asking if they know I can't play? If Mom and Dad didn't ground me all the time, they totally would have included me.

Three. Mrs. P said I need to make some more observations, so that's what I'm going to do. I'll finish my rest, grab my notebook, and when Mom and Dad get home it's easy peasy from there.

Hold up. What number am I on? I still have time to rest here, right? Right. I close my eyes and start counting again at one. . . .

"Awww, look at him, hon. He's all tuckered out," Dad whispers.

Mom's trademark sigh hisses back.

Oh no. I fell asleep on the couch.

In my underpants.

"Oooh! We should take a picture," Dad says. I resist the urge to move or shout "No! No, we shouldn't!" Maybe if I stay super still, they'll move along, and I can get out of here.

Mom must have glared or slugged him or something because he says "I'm kidding, I'm kidding. What's wrong? I can't make a joke?" On the other hand, if I open my eyes and give myself up, I could totally observe their behavior, like Mrs. P suggested.

"Do you think it's funny that he blatantly disregards what we tell him to do?" Mom's voice is so sharp she could slice bricks with it. Safer to stay put and fake sleep until she's left the room. Or calmed down. Whichever comes first.

"No, I think it's funny that he's sound asleep on the couch in his underwear."

Thanks, Dad.

"Do *not* defend him. Not today. He knows he's supposed to go straight to his room. He *knows* this. And yet he couldn't walk ten feet down the hall to his room to fall asleep? Where are his clothes?" Mom isn't giving this up. The more she talks, the madder she sounds.

"Who's defending him? Come on. Can you put yourself in the kid's shoes for one minute? Think about how you feel at the end of a long day. So he fell asleep. Big deal.

Go wake him up and send him to his room if it bothers you that much." Dad isn't giving in either.

"What bothers me is that he ignores our instructions and you don't seem to care."

"Come on, Mal. Why is this an 'all-or-nothing' situation? What is going on with you? You are so worried about being obeyed that you've lost perspective."

Mom makes one of her gasp-y, 'I'm offended'-type sounds, then everything is quiet. It's not a good quiet. It's a scary movie style, the-monster-is-about-to-jump-out-and-eat-somebody type of quiet.

I don't dare move. I imagine I'm a Jeff-shaped boulder resting at the bottom of a mountain valley. I'm a Popsicle in the freezer. A Jeff-sicle. I'm—

It's still too quiet.

Do they know I'm awake? What's going on? I listen and wait.

Silence.

I open one eye and a teeny, sideways sliver of living room appears. No Mom and Dad. Did they leave? They could be any—

SLAM.

Heavy shoes tromp down the hallway, toward the source of the sound. I hop up, grab my stinky clothes, and am in my room by the time I hear angry voices funnel down the hall.

I can't make out what they're saying, but the way they're saying it makes my insides cold. I didn't realize that something as simple as a nap could spawn this type of anger in a parent. Even worse? Mom is absolutely, definitely, a thousand percent smack dab in Guaranteed Grounding mode. If I so much as sneeze, and the sneezy droplets float underneath my bedroom door, I'm done for. Grounded until I'm 37.

How is a kid supposed to function in these conditions? I click my favorite green pen and doodle for a minute, then *haiku* to clear my throbbing head:

> Is there a way to
> Undo a bad day? Because
> I'll reset it all.

> Soccer is no fun
> Unless best friends invite you
> No luck for me though

> Oh cursed noodle
> Lying in wait on the floor
> Stupid lasagna

Zip whimpers outside in the hallway, then I hear a car pull into the drive. Sadie must be home from dance class. She doesn't know she's walking into a parental minefield.

What do I do? I know it's risky, but I have to warn her. She'd do the same for me. I wait until I hear her footsteps in the hallway and I open my door about an inch.

"Pssst! Sadie!"

I open the door wider and stand back. She walks in, slings her backpack from her shoulders, and sets it in my desk chair. "Hey. Where are Mom and Dad?"

"They're in their room. Red alert. Mom's super mad because I fell asleep on the couch." She doesn't need to know the part about my underpants.

"She's mad because you fell asleep? That's it? Are you sure? No unfortunate science experiments, dragging trash through the house, or friends over without permission?" She looks genuinely surprised.

"Nothing. I promise. I came home, laid down on the couch, and fell asleep. That was enough to start armageddon. Just wanted to give you the heads up."

"Thanks. Speaking of heads up, I heard you wiped out and cracked your head open in the lunchroom. Can I see it?" She steps around behind me, peering at my sore noggin.

Evan and Q's laughter echoes in my head. "No, cut it out." I squirm and cover the back of my head with my hands. "I'm fine. I slipped is all."

She wraps an arm around my shoulders for a quick, slightly reassuring side-hug, then she pauses and sniffs the air. "What's that weird smell? Is that burnt pizza?"

Ugh.

I gently push her away. "Lasagna. Open the window if it bugs you."

Sadie unlatches and raises the glass, and inhales. "I guess that kind of puts a big wet blanket on your making-our-parents-unground-you project, huh? What are you going to do?"

"I'll figure something out."

She takes another deep breath at the window, then sits in my desk chair. "What's the big deal about being grounded for Game Day, anyway? So you can't go. Watch it on YouTube."

"First of all, it's Gamer*Con*. Not Game *Day*. Show some respect. Second, I can't watch YouTube. Grounded, remember? And even if I could watch YouTube, I'd rather be there in person with my friends. Duh. Gaming tournaments, character appearances, author visits, fan art?"

"Sor-ry." She picks up my Rubik's cube and twists it until three rows of orange squares align. "It happens every year, right? If you miss one year you just go the next, what's the big deal?'

"What's the big deal? It's not just about GamerCon. If I don't get ungrounded, Evan and Q are going to go without me, and that will be it. No more best friends."

Zip unleashes his "somebody's at the door" barking bonanza, and the doorbell rings. Sadie's eyes bug out. "Shoot. I bet I left something in Mrs. St. John's car. Sorry." She bolts. I lie flat on my bed and listen as she answers the door.

"Hi. Um, is Jeff home?" It doesn't sound like Mrs. St. John. It's a female voice.

"He's here, but he can't come to the door. Can I tell him who stopped by?"

"Tell him Vince and Nicole hope he's doing okay," Nic says. "It looked like he hit his head pretty hard."

"Could you give him this, too?" Vince's voice says.

"Yeah, sure. I will. Thanks for checking on him," Sadie says.

"Sure. See you," Nicole says. The front door squeals and thunks closed, and a fraction of a second later, Sadie's in my doorway again.

"Do you know a Nicole and a Vince? They came to tell you they hope you're okay, and they brought you this." She hands me a hand-drawn card. On the front, it reads "get well soon," and there's a near-perfect likeness of Sergeant Sting. The inside says "Sorry about your head. Feel better. Signed, Vince and Nic"

Sadie reads over my shoulder. "Did they draw this? Your friends are talented."

"They're not my friends." I snap. "Evan and Q are."

"Oh, really? Okay." Sadie backs across the room. "Where's *their* get-well card?"

That question makes my cheeks burn, but before I can respond, Mom calls out. "Jeffrey! Come here, please!"

A hot lump of dread plunges from my throat to my stomach.

"Time to go." Sadie half walks, half trots across the hallway to her room.

I walk down the hall to the living room like Sergeant Sting tunneling under the anteater fields. One careful step at a time.

"Who was at the door?" Mom's real voice is back, not the angry voice. She pats the couch next to her.

I sit on the edge, back straight as a ruler, facing her. "Nicole and Vince."

"Why did you invite friends over when you're grounded?"

"I didn't invite anybody. They showed up." Mom has that "Mmm-hmm yeah right" expression, so I add "I promise."

That seems to satisfy her, because she asks, "Did you have a good nap?"

I nod and mentally check her expression against the Visual Guide to Parental Happiness. The good news is she's not in Guaranteed Grounding. The bad news is I'm pretty sure she's firmly in Proceed With Extreme Caution.

"Are you feeling alright?" Her voice is soft, but I'm cautious. I can almost hear the ticking doom bomb hidden beneath her gentleness.

"Yeah. I'm tired. But otherwise okay, I guess. A little headache. No big deal."

"How long were you awake on the couch?"

How long was I awake? Is this a test? I rewind my memories for a moment, trying to remember the first thing I heard. "Um, I remember Dad saying something about taking my picture. That was the first thing I heard, I think. I ran to my room as soon as you guys left."

"No, I mean before your dad and I came home."

"Before that? It—It wasn't long. Like, a couple minutes,

maybe? I didn't mean to fall asleep so fast."

"It's been a long time since you fell asleep right after school. Can you remember the last time you did that?"

I don't seem to be in trouble. Not yet, anyway. Proceed With Extreme Caution. "No. I don't remember ever doing that."

"You were in kindergarten. You fell asleep on the bus on the way home and the driver had to wake you at your stop." Her voice is far away and melty, and I relax a bit. "Turned out you had the flu."

"Huh. Well, I don't think I have the flu today." I scooch back on the couch and lean into the cushions.

"I think you're right." Mom squints and looks at me sideways. "Your Dad got a call from Nurse Traci a couple of minutes ago. Do you want to tell me what happened?"

Heat floods my face. No, I definitely do *not* want to tell her what happened. I feel like I'm flat on the cafeteria floor again and Evan and Q's laughter rings in my ears. I flush the thoughts from my brain. "What did Nurse Traci say?"

"She apologized for not calling us sooner. She said you slipped in the cafeteria and hit your head, and we need to keep an eye on you. With concussions, sometimes symptoms show up later."

All I remember about my visit to Nurse Traci is her horrible onion breath.

"Guess what the symptoms are?" A sad half-smile crawls across her face. "Sleepiness, headache, upset stomach, confusion."

"Oh. Well. My stomach's fine."

"Good, you have that going for you." Mom chuckles. "Your Dad and I think you should stay home from school tomorrow and rest."

"Now I'm confused. Why?"

"Nurse Traci said, 'if in doubt, sit it out.' You can go back on Thursday if you're feeling better, but you're home tomorrow. And no P.E. the rest of the week just in case."

"School is the one place I can see my friends. And now I can't even do that?"

"Not tomorrow you can't. You and I will spend the day at home. I'll need to work, but you need to rest your brain."

"But it was just a stupid accident! I don't need to miss school. I'm fine."

"When you hit your head, it's better to be safe than sorry. Your brain is important, kiddo. The more you rest and let it heal, the sooner you'll be back at school." She stands and stretches. "Come on, Zip, let's go outside." Zip trots to her side and they leave me slumped on the couch.

My brain feels like it's on overdrive right now. I can't go to school tomorrow, which means I can't hang out with Evan and Q, which means they'll forget me even more by the time I come back to school.

If I *really* had a head injury, would I be thinking so hard? I don't think so.

I'll be stuck at home. No friends. An entire day. Alone with Mom.

Chapter 14

Clearly, the Wednesday morning sun doesn't know I need rest. Because it's way too bright in my room for sleeping.

I roll sideways and sit up. Slowly. My head sloshes back and forth inside, heavy, like it's full of water. It doesn't hurt, but it feels tilted. Not terrible, just... not great.

Everything's so quiet and still. I've never noticed how silent our house is when it's just me and there's no YouTube. Or, I guess, when it's just me and Mom. Where is she, anyway? I wonder if she forgot about me and went to work. I pick up my trusty notebook and pen, and plod down the hall to satisfy my curiosity.

With any luck, today I'll feel good enough to do some Mom observing. Maybe that stupid slippery lasagna noodle did me a favor. If I can't be at school with my friends, I can at least make some progress with her. All I need is one thing to make Mom happy. One. And if Mom's happy, then Dad's happy. Then I get my friends back.

How hard can it be?

The kitchen smells like skunk—no, wait—that's coffee. Mom and her coffee mug are at the kitchen table, already in Full Work Mode. She's hunched behind her laptop. All I can see is the top of her head and the points of her elbows. From where I'm standing it looks like the laptop sprouted a pair of Mom-colored wings.

What can I observe about her behavior? I open my notebook and write:

> Mom Encounter: Wednesday, ??:?? AM. Kitchen.
> 1) Posture reminds me of the stealth mission round in Fire Ant Heroes 3.
> a. Is she waiting to pounce?
> b. Or is she going to help me?

In FAH3, I talk to a character so I can find out if they're going to help me or hurt me. In real life, I need breakfast first.

I open the pantry and grab a box of Frooty O's. At the sound of the pantry door, Mom pops up from behind the laptop.

"Morning. How are you feeling?"

"Weird." I plunge my hand into the Frooty O box. "Tiny headache. Mostly, I hunger."

Mom looks like she's trying to solve a word problem without showing her work. I know this face because I've made it. "Okay. Good. Hunger is a good sign. Let's get you cozy on the couch, where I can keep an eye on you." She plucks the cereal box out of my hands and returns it to the counter. Before I can say anything she says, "I'll bring you breakfast. Today is all about you getting rest."

She ushers me to the couch. I nestle into the cushions and Mom tucks a blanket around my legs and feet. "See? Nice and cozy."

She's not wrong. It's warm and kind of snuggly and I don't exactly hate it. Mom's phone dings. She scowls, then thumbs the phone screen, texting something fast and furious. "No tv, though," she adds, without looking up.

"I know."

I know she's supposed to be "at work" and all, but would it kill her to look at me when she talks to me? Also, what about breakfast? Didn't she say she was going to bring me breakfast? She could have at least let me keep the Frooty-O box.

Mom zombie-walks, staring at her phone until she gets to her laptop, then she sits and stares at that.

Is the concussion messing with my head? Because I want Mom to keep talking with me. And I don't think it's just because she forgot my food. "Hey Mom?"

"Mmm?" Her eyes are forward, fingers flying across the keys.

Um. . . . "Do you like Frooty O's?" Maybe she'll get the hint.

"It's not my favorite, but I like it fine." Tap, tap tap, tap. "I didn't eat any of your cereal if that's what you're getting at."

"No, no. I was just wondering if, um. . ." I give her a second to fill in the blanks. *Come on, Mom. Rhymes with shmek-fest? Nothing.*

Mom's glassy eyes look like they belong on one of Sadie's old dolls. "Sorry hon, I've got a meeting to get ready for. I'll check on you in a little while, okay?"

"No breakfast?" Hollow disappointment sinks into my gut.

"Oh! Um, yes, of course, I promise." She looks at her watch. "I'm so sorry, sweetheart. I have to hop on a quick video chat with my boss and then I'll bring you something to eat." She exhales loudly, fluffs her hair, and clicks a button. Suddenly she's like a different person. Her eyes are wide and her voice is bright, full of energy. If she wasn't so old, she could be a YouTuber.

I tug my notebook and pen out from beneath my fluffy blanket and jot down a few notes.

> Wednesday, continued
> Tucks me in on the couch and promises breakfast
> Forgets she promised me breakfast
> Is easily distracted by texts
> Poofs up her hair for the video chat.

I lay in my nest on the couch, listening to Mom's boss string a bunch of words together. Mom chirps happy statements every once in a while, like "absolutely!" And "of course we can!" and "I'm on it!" When I peek at her, she looks like she's ready to leap into action. She's like a real estate marketing superhero in lounge pants.

The call ends and the house is quiet again. Regular Mom reappears. She clicks buttons on her laptop and types away like crazy.

The Frooty-O box is on the counter, taunting me. It's like, "Hey, Jeff. I remember you. Your mom doesn't. Bwah ha ha."

It's not like I'm home recovering from head trauma or anything.

Is this what Mrs. Peddy meant when she said what people do is more important than what they say? The only reason Mom's home from work is to take care of me, right? So why am I still hungry?

I pick up my pen and *haiku*.

> Mom said she'd feed me
> I guess she meant after work
> So I'm on my own

> How will Mom behave
> If I interrupt her work
> For some cereal?

> Haiku writing is
> Harder than it looks sometimes
> But I keep trying

Bongo drumming pounds the air and I almost drop my notebook. Mom's ringtone startles me every time.

"Hey." It must be Dad. She wouldn't answer a work call with "hey." There's a long pause while she listens to whatever Dad is saying. I take this opportunity to prop myself up on the couch for a better view.

"You know I'm home with Jeff today. You can't make it to a fast-food drive-through or something?" She drops her hand and leans back, facing the ceiling. "I get it, I do, but I don't feel good about dragging him on an errand. What about Rob? Couldn't he pick a sandwich up for you?"

Mom stands and shoves her chair backward. She pulls in a slow, deep breath. "That's not fair. I don't mind helping you. I'm trying to work today too, remember? I've got a staff meeting, then comps to pull, and a showing to prep for, and uncooperative owners, and—" Whatever Dad says next is not the right thing to say, because she smacks the edge of the table. "Fine. I'll drop it off in an hour."

She makes a growling, frustrated sound. "Jeff?" That's a "come in here now Jeff" if I've ever heard one. I know she's not mad at me, but the edge in her voice makes my palms sweat. I sit up slowly and shuffle into the kitchen.

Mom has the fridge open and her torso is halfway inside. I scoot past her, pick up the Frooty-O box, and commence snacking. Finally. "Yeah?"

"Your dad forgot his lunch and he can't get away to come pick it up." She straightens up and takes a half step back. She scrutinizes the fridge shelves for a few seconds, then pulls out Dad's lunch bag and a 20-ounce bottle of soda. "I have to run this over to his office, because apparently I have nothing else going on and if I did, it isn't more important than lunch."

Is this sarcasm? Mom hates sarcasm. I'm confused. "So. . . you're leaving me here?" If she's driving all the way over to Dad's office, she'll be gone for almost a whole hour. That's a whole hour's worth of time that I'm about to miss. You know, for research. All because Dad forgot his lunch.

Mom whirls around to face me, shaking Dad's soda in the process. "I won't be long, I promise. You know who to call in an emergency, right?"

"Mrs. Fischer?" I shrug.

Mom does that thing where she lowers her chin and raises her eyebrows, so I *really* know I'm wrong. "No. In an emergency, you call 9-1-1. How's your head?"

"My head is fine. It's just. . . ."

"What?" Mom collects her purse and keys, but she fixes her eyes on me. "What's wrong?'

What's wrong? Maybe it's the swimmy feeling in my head, maybe the weird pull of wanting Mom to stick around gets to me, or maybe it's the Frooty-O's. What is with me? I can feel the words in my mouth, but I don't say them. No eleven-year-old tells their mom "Please don't go." But no kid in their right mind—of any age—says what comes out of my mouth next:

"I'm bored."

A terrible light flashes in her eyes. "You're *bored*?"

I desperately want to take back those two words. I can't. If you say something and make an angry Mom, you're stuck with her. All you can do is nod and deal with the fallout as best you can.

"Bored." She says it again, like she can't believe this word came out of my mouth.

That makes two of us, Mom.

My brain spins like a hamster wheel and my heart hammers in my chest. How do I fix this situation? "Maybe I can come with you? For some company?"

Mom balances Dad's lunch bag on top of her purse, grips the soda bottle in one hand and her keys in the other. She hustles down the hall to the garage door with quick, short steps, barking at me over her shoulder. "No no, if you're bored now, do you know how awful riding in a car will be? You'd be trapped with me for a whole forty-five minutes."

She opens the door and pauses for a moment. Then, like something out of a scary movie, she turns toward me. *Extra slowly.* Oh, boy. I spy a Mom who is perched on the uppermost edge of the Steer Clear stage. "Since you're well enough to feel bored, I'll help you keep busy: Give Zip a bath, and load the dishwasher. Is that enough to do, or do you think you'll still be bored?"

"That's plenty, but—" I really shouldn't say the next thought in my head. Should I?

"But what?"

"Never mind."

"Just tell me, please. I need to get going."

"Do you really want me to do these chores? Aren't I supposed to be resting?" My voice comes out smaller and whinier than I intended.

"Yes, I do. And yes, you are. But that's boring, right?" A bitter smirk creeps across her face. "Take care of those chores before I get back, and then we'll see how you're feeling." She slams the door behind her.

My head swims and throbs, and I feel like punching something, crying, and screaming all at the same time. What just happened? I wanted to hang out with Mom, test my hypothesis and maybe win a little freedom back. Instead, I launched her face-first into Guaranteed Grounding. What is it about b-o-r-e-d that makes parents insane?

What in the world am I supposed to do now? It's like she completely forgot why I am at home from school in the first place. This is brain-resting time, not dog-washing, dishwasher-loading time. Ugh. How much do you want to bet that by the time she gets home, my brain will be fried like an egg?

Zip trots to my side and stares up at me with his giant brown eyes. His tail swishes side to side. It's almost like he recognized the word "b-a-t-h" and he's ready to go.

"Okay, buddy, hang on," I tell him. "I gotta do the dishes first." Bathing a dog this cute? Maybe not the worst punishment in the world. But missing out on quality time to regain my freedom?

That stings.

Chapter 15

By the time Mom's keys rattle in the kitchen door, I have all my chores done and I'm back in my couch-nest. I squeeze my eyes shut and listen for familiar footsteps. There's a rustle of paper and the smack of Mom's purse on the countertop. A familiar fried aroma wafts into the living room and my stomach growls.

My concussion head churns with questions. Is Mom still upset with me? How can I salvage what's left of this day? Did I rinse the tub after Zip's bath? Do I smell fries?

If she's still in Steer Clear, what could I do that would calm her down? Maybe it would be a smarter move to act like she never got mad. I could try something like saying, *"What's for lunch? What would you say to taking me and my friends to GamerCon?"*

Ugh. Why am I so nervous about talking with my own mom? I'm making this harder than it needs to be.

"Are you still bored?" Mom's sitting on the edge of the coffee table. I swallow hard and—slowly, because it still kinda hurts—shake my head.

"Good." She sounds calm. My shoulders deflate a little. I catch a salty whiff of fast food and the scent makes my mouth water. I spot a Jim Junior's Burger Joint bag in her lap and smile. She smiles back. "Were you able to rest at all?"

"Not really. I just finished my chores and laid down a minute ago."

She hands me a wrapped cheeseburger and a greasy paper tray loaded with cheesed potatoes.

"Thanks."

Then, Mom says something I haven't heard her say in maybe ever. "I'm sorry I forgot your breakfast. And I'm really sorry I lost my temper earlier."

Before I can say anything, my nose tingles, and tears spill onto my unwrapped cheeseburger.

Of all the things to cry over, why do I cry over Mom being sorry?

"Everybody loses their temper. No big deal."

One of the fries has too much cheese on it so I focus on removing the extra. It's not like I had wanted to spend the day with Mom anyway. I had wanted to be at school with my friends.

"Aw, honey." She passes me an extra napkin and I dry my face. "Do you want to talk about it?"

"It's okay." Suddenly I'm not hungry anymore. I dump my burger and fries back in the bag and roll it tight. "My stomach's upset. I just want to sleep for a little while."

"Of course." She tucks the blanket around my shoulders. "Hope you feel better, kiddo. Love you." Her voice and the fleecy blanket wrap around me. I nestle deeper into the couch and drift to sleep.

HOW TO RAISE HAPPY PARENTS
by JEFF PENNANT

CHAPTER TWO

OBSERVATION SESSION – RESEARCH NOTES

SUBJECT: MOM

*Note—at the time of this research, author/scientist is recovering from a concussion which may or may not affect said research.

Mom Encounter: Wednesday, ??:?? AM. Kitchen.

1) Posture reminds me of the stealth mission round in Fire Ant Heroes 3.

    a. Is she waiting to pounce?

b. Or is she going to help me?

2) Tucks me in on the couch and promises breakfast

3) Forgets she promised me breakfast

4) Is easily distracted by texts

5) Fluffs her hair for the video chat

6) During video chat, could pass for (much older) YouTuber—more energy, friendlier, brighter (in between Somewhat and Full Happy)

7) Still no food

8) Dad calls -> status dropped from Somewhat Happy to Proceed With Extreme Caution

9) New stimulus: confession of boredom -> Guaranteed Grounding -> extra chores

10) Surprise apology

INTERPRETATION OF FINDINGS:

I went into my research today with an open (also sore and headachy) mind. My goal was to observe Mom. What makes her happy? What makes her mad? These clues will help me figure out how to move my parents from Guaranteed Grounding to Full Happy—and see my friends again.

HAPPY: This is a tough one. Today I only saw Mom happy when she tucked me in on the couch and when she brought me lunch. Even if I wanted to, I can't lay on the couch all day every day, or eat 24/7. So this doesn't help a lot.

MAD: When Mom had to take Dad his lunch, that made her mad. It's kind of nice that she's upset with someone else for a change. Does she get this angry when I forget my lunch? (Note to self: Remember lunch.)

This is already a known fact among kids, but it's a fact worth repeating: No matter how bored you are, never, ever, ever, ever tell your parent. Once I said b-o-r-e-d, Mom vaulted from Somewhat Happy to Steer Clear in record time. No stars on Yelp. Do not recommend.

BOTH HAPPY AND MAD: My mom's job seems complicated. Sometimes she seems grumpy about it. Other times, like when they video chat, it seems exciting. I'm not sure. Either way, she was so focused on her phone and her laptop she forgot to bring me breakfast. What was so important that she couldn't take a second to feed her head-injured son? I'm not feeling sorry for myself, I'm documenting my research.

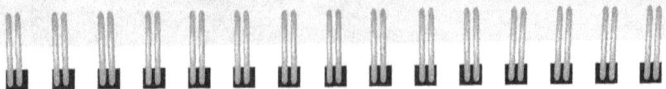

BONUS STUFF: My mom apologized. To me. This might be the first time in my life to experience this. Maybe leaving the house helped Mom cool off a little? Or maybe Mom just likes driving? Driving may be the grown-up version of being sent to your room. Like, it could kind of be a punishment but it's really not that terrible once you're there. In Mom's case, more driving might be good.

Concussions are bad. They make you feel like a giant pudding head, and it's super hard to think, talk, write, or do anything when you have one. For example, the sentence you just read? That took me 27 minutes to write. Also, I should have waited until my head felt better before I tried to observe anything, much less write about it.

If you have the choice, don't get a concussion.

Chapter 17

Thanks to a good night's sleep and an actual full day of resting, I'm happy to report I'm feeling back to my awesome self again.

School wasn't awesome at all, though. I had to spend lunch in the library getting caught up on the work I missed. Don't get me wrong—I love the library. But I didn't get to see Evan and Q. I didn't even get to see Nic or Vince—which isn't that big of a deal, but I wanted to ask why they came by my house the other day.

So between making up school work and catching up on FAH3 graphic novels, I barely had any time to eat lunch today. A guy can't be expected to be at his best when he's fueled by a handful of baby carrots.

I'm still supposed to go straight to my room when I get home. But by the time I get off the bus after school, I'm having a hunger emergency. I'm pretty sure my stomach has digested itself. Do I take a chance and head for the kitchen? Or should I play it safe and go straight to my room?

Hunger pains stab me in the belly. There's my answer.

Me and my starving belly run straight to the "approved after-school snack" jar.

A while back, Mom bought a huge glass canister and stocks it regularly with veggie chips. Yep. We're Those People. Even though they taste like sandpaper, I'm actually looking forward to veggie chips. I'm *that* hungry. And, of course, today the jar is empty.

I check the cupboard for backup snacks. Maybe we have granola bars? Nope.

I check the fridge. Are you a fan of unidentifiable leftovers and expired milk? Me neither.

Last chance—the pantry. Flour, baking soda, something called evaporated milk—what?—and a few cans of corn. Ugh. Wait. I spy a box of dry spaghetti and a can of meat sauce. My stomach roars its choice. I must make spaghetti and meat sauce.

I toss the ingredients into a glass bowl, shove it in the microwave, and hit the "dinner plate" button six times. That ought to do it. I perform a hunger dance and watch the microwave timer count down while I wait.

At two minutes left, the garage door grumbles, and Zip races to the door.

Somebody's home.

My snack isn't done. There's no way I'm going to make it to my room in time. I'm busted.

Zip's tail thumps against the wall. My heart pounds right along with it. But my stomach? Empty stomach doesn't care about my parents. Empty stomach wants spaghetti.

One minute, thirty seconds left. Keys jangle in the door. My parents' voices say hello to Zip. Dad's voice drifts down the hallway, but Mom's slices through the house. "Ew. Zip, you stink. Would someone please, for the love of Pete, give Zip another bath." A *thud* as she drops her work bags in the hallway. Now Mom's muttering words I can't quite make out from in here. They probably have something to do with me being grounded until the end of time.

One minute left. Even from down the hall, Mom's grumpy voice sounds the way an elbow jab feels in your ribs. Sharp and uncomfortable. If I had to guess, her face has Proceed With Extreme Caution all over it. I'll get a visual confirmation on this as soon as I can. My belly is wound tight – maybe from impending doom, maybe from relentless hunger, it's hard to tell.

"Jeff?" she says. *Jab.*

Thirty seconds left. "Yes?" *Stall, Jeff.*

She sighs like it's her last exhale before climbing Everest. "What are you doing out of your room?"

You knew this was coming. Stay calm and take your time. I wish I had my notebook. I'd write Proceed With Extreme Caution. Because I was right. That's exactly where she is on the scale.

"Well? Answer me, please." Both hands are planted on her hips.

"I was hungry?" I don't know why I asked. It's not a question. It's factual accuracy. I am hungry.

"Hungry," she repeats. I nod. She raises her chin and holds her hand like she's stopping traffic. "What's that smell?"

Eeeeeeeep screeches the microwave. Before I can move, Mom opens the door and peeks into the cloudy, smelly appliance. She is firmly wedged between me and my food. My steaming, sauce-splattered food.

When she turns around, I can't tell if she's impressed or stunned silent. Her jaw is slack, eyes narrow. She's twisted the end of her shirt so hard that the left side is in a knot. Which is weird because it's one of her nice work shirts.

My stomach growls. "I was hungry." This time it wasn't a question.

Mom stands, her eyes trained laser-sharp on me. "Sadie! Come help your brother set the table for dinner."

"It's dinnertime?" I expected to get sent back to my room, not enlisted in the dinner prep army. My belly rumbles approval, but the rest of me? Confused. I don't see any takeout containers.

Mom stands in the center of the kitchen, barking orders like a general.

"Change of plans. Pour a glass of water for everybody."

"But Mom—"

"Get. Water. Now."

I grab four glasses from the cabinet. Sadie flutters around the table with plates and forks. She shoots me an exclamation mark face that says, *you're an idiot!* I respond with question mark shrugs like *just lucky I guess?* Then I deal napkins like playing cards to each empty seat, with an extra for myself.

Yeah, this is awkward. But look at me. I don't know how, but I'm still out of my room.

Mom half places, half drops a half-empty jar of applesauce on the kitchen table then yells at the ceiling. "Matt! Time to eat!"

Are we eating my snack? All four of us? *My* snack?

She dumps little heaps of my spaghetti onto each plate, then drops into her chair.

I sit next to her, wishing I had my notebook.

Dad strides in, sniffing the air. He's changed from his work clothes into his "I'm a Blood Donor" t-shirt and elastic waistband lounge pants. "Kinda early for dinner, isn't it?"

Nobody answers.

He sits at his usual seat and bows his head, so we all do too. "Lord, thank You for the food before us, the family beside us, and the love between us. Amen."

I shovel semi-warm, mostly-cooked spaghetti into my mouth so fast I barely taste the sauce. Dad blinks at the noodle pile on his plate. "What is this?"

"Jeff made dinner for everybody, didn't you, Jeff?" Mom replies.

"Apparently."

"You cooked this by yourself? Stove, microwave, or campfire?' Dad asks, fork in hand.

"Dad." I chew a clump of noodles like it's a beef jerky

stick.

"Can I ask what inspired your sudden helpfulness?" Judging by the skeptical look on his face, Dad thinks I'm about to poison him.

I open my mouth to answer but Mom beats me to it. "You might recall that our son is grounded. He's supposed to come home after school and stay in his room."

"Yes, I was there." Dad plucks a stick of uncooked pasta from his food pile and sets it aside. Then he loads a fork and takes a bite. Muffled *crunch crack crunch* sounds float across the table.

"While you were changing clothes, I found him in the kitchen and this in the microwave." She points to the sticky stack of noodles on her plate.

Dad gulps a mouthful of water and nods approvingly. "Sauce is alright. Thanks, Jeff."

"You're welcome."

Mom sits back in her chair and crosses her arms. "You're okay with him ignoring the fact that he's grounded?"

"We grounded him, Mal, we're not running Guantanamo. If the kid's hungry after school, I think he should make himself a snack. But—and I'm very serious about this—no using the stove or open flames. Grab food and get straight to your room, okay pal?"

"Okay." We sit in silence for a while. Well, mostly silence. There's a lot of crunching.

I nudge Sadie's foot under the table. She nudges back

and gives me a question mark face.

I mouth "What's Gua-ma-ma-ma?"

She mouths back "Prison." I nod, and she eats her applesauce.

The circles under Mom's eyes are as dark as her mood. If I had my reference chart handy, I would double-check, but it sure looks like she's in Steer Clear territory. Not. Good.

I scan Dad's face. Blank. Quiet. He seems to have moved on, oblivious to Mom's simmering. He's slurping spaghetti like it's his job. Mom is glaring at him and breathing deep and slow.

When Sadie and I were little, we used to actually have fun at family meals. Sometimes we'd take turns playing jokes or making up silly word games with Mom and Dad.

I don't know when the change happened, exactly, but now things are different. Night after night, there's always something. Work is awful. Traffic is the worst. Gas is expensive. Blah, blah, blah everything's super bad. Sometimes Mom and Dad will ask about school, but mostly Sadie and I sit in silence, eat, and listen to my parents complain.

"Traffic was miserable today, huh?" Dad says. He rambles on about highway construction and toll roads. While he's talking, I c a r e f u l l y study him and Mom. For research.

Dad's body might be sitting at the dinner table, but his brain is still at the corner of 168th and Dodge Street. I have no idea where Mom's brain is, but the rest of her? Does not look comfortable.

"You remember the workshop I spent three months putting together?" Mom stabs noodles with her fork and drags them through sauce.

"Mmm-hmmm." Dad scrapes the bottom of the applesauce jar like he's digging for gold.

"Three months of my life, working on one project." Mom's voice wobbles. "*Amy's* presenting it tomorrow to her prospective clients."

"That's great! Good for her."

Mom slams her fork against the table. "No! Not great! You don't get it. She stole my work and she's presenting like the whole thing is hers. She previewed it today for the director. He loved it. Now she's probably going to get Marketer of the Month. With *my project*." She shoves her plate aside and drops her chin in her hands. Sadie and I exchange glances.

Dad dabs the corner of his mouth with his napkin. "Wait. How did she get your presentation, exactly?"

"I saved it in my folder on the company drive."

"Are you sure it's your presentation? Did she ask you if she could use it?"

Mom sighs. "Yes, I'm sure it's mine. If she'd asked permission beforehand, I probably would have worked something out with her. I don't mind sharing." Her voice cracks. "But I do mind stealing. You just don't do that to your colleagues."

"Collies?" I whisper to Sadie.

"No. Coll-eagues. Co-workers." She whispers back.

A scowl creeps across my face. Somebody's stealing from my mom? That's no good.

"Did you say something to the director and let him know it's your work? That you were the one who created the workshop?"

Mom's shoulders slumped. "No. I was too stunned and mad to say anything."

"That's awful. I'm so sorry, hon," Dad says.

Mom looks like she has more to say, but no words are coming out. Sadie and Dad stare at their plates.

I watch Mom. My heart thumps extra hard, like it's trying to get my brain's attention. *Thump-THUMP. Hey YOU. Hey YOU.*

Tears stream down her face, which is as red as the tomato sauce on her plate.

Thump-THUMP. Do SOMEthing. Do SOMEthing.

So I do what any responsible son would do when his mom is crying. I clear my throat and start talking. In a made-up accent.

"Paws der peppahr, pliss." Sadie groans and hands me the pepper shaker. She might think I'm an idiot, but I know how to get a giggle out of Sadie. Usually, anyway.

Mom looks up from her plate. Is she smiling? "Not now, Jeff." *No, she's not smiling.* She has plummeted into Guaranteed Grounding.

Thump-THUMP. Do SOMEthing. Can anybody else hear my heart beating? I need to make her laugh. Or at least change the conversation. I try my favorite accent, the one that never fails to crack a smile, The Vintage Cowboy.

"Heeey, y'all. Haow dee-id yoo lahk mah sper-geddy?"

Dad drops his chin to his chest and shakes his head. That's how proud he is.

Nobody says anything. I'm pretty sure there's no more sound in the entire world. Except maybe my thudding heart. I glance across the table at Mom.

What I see isn't good. She's crossed her arms and is face down on the table. *THUMP-THUMP.*

That's it. I'm going all out. Pennants don't do anything halfway. I try Jar-Jar Binks.

"Eeef-a you-sa so miserable at-a you work, why-sa you don't gets-sa a deefferent job?"

Mom and Dad push their chairs away from the table at the exact same time. If I didn't know better, I'd think they'd practiced this move for weeks. It's spooky. Sadie's eyes get huge.

I cough and speak in my own voice, which sounds tiny compared to Jar-Jar's. "You know, maybe try something that you actually like for a change?"

Mom sobs into her hands.

Dad sighs. Then, "Jeff, I think dinner is over. You can go back to your room."

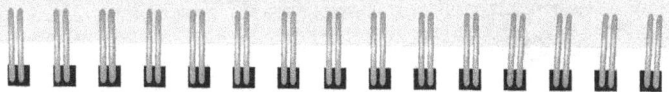

HOW TO RAISE HAPPY PARENTS
by JEFF PENNANT

CHAPTER THREE

It's important, as scientists, that we are aware of the risks involved in our research. There is an element of danger in any experiment. Especially when it comes to observing parents in the field. Today's session wasn't planned, but I hoped it might be helpful. It ended up being hazardous and more than a little confusing.

OBSERVATION SESSION

Monday, 4:31 pm

Kitchen*

*Observer was extremely hungry

STATUS:

DAD: Somewhat Happy

MOM: Proceed With Extreme Caution

NOTES:

1) While I was making a snack, Mom and Dad came home
2) Mom was mad because I wasn't in my room (also because Zip smells like a dog)
   a. Punishment for not being in my room = sharing my snack with the whole family.
3) Dad appreciated early dinner
   a. He said if I need a snack, get it fast and go to my room.
   b. This sent Mom->Steer Clear
   c. Dad complimented my cooking skills
4) Dad complained about traffic
5) Mom complained about work
   a. Dad asked questions
   b. Mom said a lady stole her ideas->Guaranteed Grounding
   c. I offered silly voices and helpful career advice
   d. Mom cried.
   e. Dad sent me to my room.

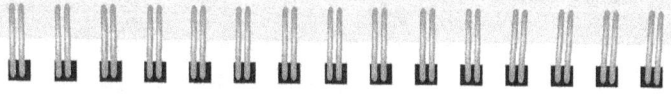

INTERPRETATION OF FINDINGS:

As I stated earlier, I'm confused.

Dad hung out in Somewhat Happy, even when Mom cried. Nothing bothered him. How? Why? Could he have been that happy because I (accidentally) made dinner? That doesn't seem likely. Crunchy noodles aren't good.

I knew getting a snack would be dicey, but I didn't expect Mom to be *that* mad about it. Then she nose-dived from Steer Clear into Guaranteed Grounding when she started talking about a lady stealing her ideas at work. It was kind of startling how fast that happened.

Something was different about this Guaranteed Grounding, too. Mom wasn't just mad. She had sad in between layers of mad. She was a sad/mad sandwich with grumpy bread.

Seeing Mom like that grabbed my insides and yanked me around. I wanted to do something to fix whatever was hurting her, but I didn't know how. For once, I wasn't the only reason she was upset. But even though I tried my best to help, I think I ended up making things way worse.

A lot of the data today was weird and confusing.

I don't understand why someone would steal work from my mom and say it's their own. That's not just stealing, that's lying and stealing. It's a double whammy of wrongness.

I don't understand why Mom took my food and gave it to everybody without asking me first. Isn't that kind of stealing too?

Mom and Dad usually laugh when I talk with a made-up accent. Why didn't it help this time?

I only suggested Mom get a new job because I wanted to help. Why did that make her cry so hard?

Why was Dad able to stay in Somewhat Happy even while he complained, and Mom was so sad? What's his secret? And how can I pass it along to Mom without making her cry more?

I started this book with four questions, and I'm not sure I'm any closer to figuring them out. If I don't solve these problems soon, I'm going to lose my friends.

1) Why do parents get angry?

So far, I'd say there are lots of reasons. Traffic. Thieves. Questions from their kid.

2) What can kids do to make them happy?

We can cross funny accents and spaghetti dinner off the list.

3) How fast can they switch from Guaranteed Grounding to Full Happy?

I don't know about that, but they can drop from Proceed With Extreme Caution to Guaranteed Grounding in a matter of minutes.

4) What will it take to do that?

That's the biggest question. I learned today that trying to make Mom laugh when she's upset can backfire in a hurry.

So what *can* I do?

When was the last time I saw Mom and Dad happy? Like, Full Happy happy?

It's been a long time. Months, I think.

It was Mom's birthday. We went to church that morning, then Shenanigan's for lunch (Mom's favorite). Afterward, we gave Mom her birthday gifts (Sadie made her a necklace and I painted an awesome rock paperweight), then Sadie and I put on a show we made up just for her. We sang a duet, acted out a little play, and finished with a big dance number. Mom and Dad both cheered and laughed. We had Full Happy parents and it was spectacular.

What if I made Mom and Dad a present? Mom was really upset today because somebody took something important from her. Maybe giving something back to her would help her be happy. Dad, too.

But what could I give them?

It can't be another painted rock paperweight. I know parents love them, and they're amazing, but I've already made Mom and Dad two paperweights each. There's such a thing as Too Much of a Good Thing.

What about another show? It needs to be super impressive, like a real professional stage play. Maybe Sadie could design me a cool-looking costume. We'd have to have a real stage, like the one in our school auditorium, so of course, I'd have to build that. Then we'd want a spotlight, and we'd definitely want music.

But wait. Is there time to build a stage properly? No. Would Dad let me use his power tools? That's not likely. Something tells me this project would cause more problems than it solves.

Mom's birthday show was all about celebrating Mom and all her Mom-ness. She and Dad both loved it. They love me too, right? What if, instead of a great big Mom and Dad show, I do a smaller-but-still-incredible-Jeff show?

It could be like a special tour that reminds them what an amazing son they have. Tour de Jeff. I wouldn't even need to build a stage – I could do it all in my room. That would blow their minds. They've been pretty cool about giving me my personal space. How happy would they be to really get a good look inside, you know, where the awesomeness really happens? I could give them an exclusive insider tour of my room, show them some of my favorite things (I have a few), and they won't be able to resist it. It'll be like, a giant avalanche of Full Happy tumbling over Mom and Dad.

This could work.

They'll love it. It's failproof.

EXPERIMENT IDEA:
HYPOTHESIS: When I give Mom and Dad a tour of my room, they will be reminded of my awesomeness, overwhelmed with happiness, and unground me immediately.

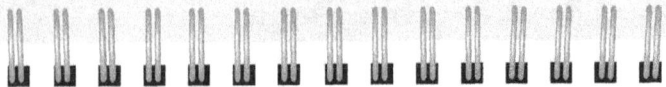

OTHER THOUGHTS:

1) Stock my own pantry. Bad things happen when a kid misses his after-school snack. From now on, I'll use some of my birthday money to buy a few snacks to keep in my room.

2) Prepare. Dinner conversation is trickier than I thought. I need to find topics that can distract them without upsetting them. Here's a short list of possibilities: Gravity, Recycling, Composting, Helpful Insect Species, and Sports.

3) Avoid accents. In tense dinnertime situations, it's probably best to keep this kind of talent to yourself.

Chapter 19

Sadie opens my bedroom door a crack. "Psst!" She tosses a packaged Big Darlin' Snack Cake across the room into my lap. "Thought you might want dessert."

"You thought right." I unwrap the oversized, oversweet cupcake. "Come in if you want." I break the giant cupcake into two chunks and hand one of the chunks to Sadie as she walks past.

She sits at my desk chair and points at the open notebook on the bed next to me. "What'cha doing?"

"Working on my field guide."

"Oh, yeah? How's that going?" She nibbles one corner of the chocolatey treat.

Where do I even start to answer that question? "I've had a couple of setbacks. I collected a lot of information tonight, though. I think I'm ready to try an experiment."

"What kind of experiment?"

I tap the notebook cover with my pen as I think. How much can I share with Sadie? "I'm still working out the details, but it's going to be cool."

She sets the half-eaten cupcake chunk on my desk and wipes her hands down the sides of her jeans. "What kind of details? Tell me. I like science too."

"Well, yeah, but there's a difference between *liking* science and *being* a scientist. Kind of like there's a difference between appreciating art and being an artist. Two different things."

"I get it. But maybe I can help." She scoots the desk chair closer to me. "It never hurts to have another set of eyes on your work, whether you're a scientist or an artist or anything else."

If Sadie reads my field guide, she might make my life miserable. She also might steal my ideas and write her own book. But she might be helpful. In her own way. I mean, she's older than me so she's known Mom and Dad longer. She might catch something I missed. Maybe.

I pick up my notebook. "If—*if*—I let you read this, you can't share it with another soul. It's top secret. Deal?"

"Of course. Deal." She takes the notebook out of my hands like it could shatter any second.

While Sadie reads, I polish off the last few bites of my cupcake. Part of me wants her to be amazed and impressed. I mean, I'm her awesome little bro and she shouldn't be surprised if what I write is total genius. Because it is.

The other part of me? That tiny part's thinking she'll get bored after the first page and ask me to summarize. Or she'll laugh and tease me. It'll be the lasagna incident all over again.

But she doesn't laugh. She keeps going. When she finally closes the notebook, she looks up at me with eyes so big you'd think she found a puppy. "Are you kidding me? You're really going to let them in here?"

"Yep. What do you think?" I brace myself for laughter and teasing.

Sadie tilts her head back and spins slowly in the chair, side to side, left to right. "When was the last time Mom and Dad were in your room?"

We sit in silence for at least a minute, thinking hard. Then I remember. "It was the summer before first grade. Pretty sure that was the last time."

"Oh yeah!" Sadie plants her feet and sits up straight. "Mom cleaned your room one morning while you were at science camp." She grins. "You were so mad."

"Well, yeah. I mean, it wasn't fair." My chest puffs up a little at the thought. "Mom and Dad always said their room was off-limits when we played. How come my room was fair game?"

Sadie shrugged.

"And she didn't clean. Remember? She destroyed my Lego spaceship. I had worked on it for weeks. And she crushed it."

"She tripped over it. It was an accident. You rebuilt it, right?"

"Yeah. Anyway. That was what, five years ago?"

"It's been five years since they've seen all... this." Sadie holds an arm out and twirls in the chair. "But seriously. If this is an experiment, don't you need a whatsathingy, neutron group or something?"

"Do you mean control group? Yeah. Normally. But this is kind of an emergency experiment. I mean, GamerCon is in three days."

"You've got a lot riding on this tour, then." She plants her feet on the carpet and sits straighter. "Good luck."

Luck? I don't need luck. "It's gonna be epic. They're gonna be like—plew!" I close my fists, then open them into jazz hands. "Minds. Blown."

"Sure, sure. But you might want to clean up a little, don't you think? It kinda smells weird in here."

"All part of the charm."

Sadie laughs, then she leans forward, and gets that Big Sister look. "I thought you were super sweet, the way you tried to help cheer Mom up at dinner. Even if your accents were pfffffft. Terrible." She gives me a thumbs-down.

I laugh. "Um, thanks?"

"You remember when we were little and I lost Ginger at the grocery store? My favorite doll. I was sooo upset. Like, I couldn't stop crying. Do you remember what you did for me?"

"I think so. I made you a doll out of Legos."

"Yeah! It was so sweet of you. You worked so hard to make me feel better. That's kind of like what you did for Mom. Or what you tried to do, anyway."

I remember Mom's red, teary face and my chest tightens a little. "I had to do something."

Sadie wheels close to me again. "Yeah, it was hard to see, wasn't it? I think, though, sometimes people need to lose it. They need to cry. It's okay. Every once in a while, you have to let big feelings out, so they don't, like, swallow you up. I think that's all Mom was doing." She reaches over and squeezes my shoulder.

Sadie picks her cupcake remnants off my desk and drops them in the trash. "Anyway, I hope a tour of your room is just what she needs." She leaves, closing my bedroom door behind her.

I hope so too.

I hope Mom and Dad will be so happy, so impressed with me, they'll unground me on the spot. I hope, I hope. A fizzy tingle of encouragement lifts me a little. It will all be okay.

Oh, please, God, let it all be okay.

Chapter 20

I'm so excited to tell Evan and Q about my failproof strategy I can hardly wait for lunch today. They're going to be as excited as I am. When I'm ungrounded, we're going to have a blast at GamerCon. And everyplace else. We'll be the unstoppable team again.

But by the time lunch rolls around and my class gets to the cafeteria, there are already like, 300 fifth graders talking, eating, waiting in line. My class is the last group to arrive.

I scan the room, looking for signs of Evan and Q. Our usual table is full, but they aren't there. I check our backup table next to the dessert counter. No luck. Where are they?

Nic and Vince stand up and wave at me. They're at a corner table with a couple of smiling, laughing kids I've never seen before. I haven't talked to either of them since the Lasagna Incident. My memory of that day is pretty much purple leggings, paper towels, and the sound of laughter.

One last look around the crowded room tells me

they're not at school today. I twist my paper lunch bag. For some reason, I don't have it in me to make small talk with kids I don't know, or with Nic and Vince either. I just want a chance to talk to my best friends. The thought of chit-chat with anybody but Evan and Q makes my brain itch.

Sometimes if a kid isn't feeling well, the lunch monitor will let them have quiet time in their classroom. I wade through the crowd of kids toward the main doors where Mr. Paul stands.

"Mr. Paul?" I yell over the noise.

He bends down, cups an ear, and nods, like 'go ahead.'

"Can I eat my lunch in my classroom today?"

He nods and holds a door open for me.

"Thanks." I retreat from the cafeteria and head back to Mrs. Peddy's room. The door is unlocked, the lights are off, and Mrs. P is nowhere to be seen. My desk chair is still warm when I sit, almost like I never left.

Okay, so it's not lunch with Evan and Q, but also? It's not the noisy cafeteria without Evan and Q. Score. Kind of.

At least I have quiet time to work out the details of my failproof plan.

I open my lunch and bite into a soft, cold, bologna and cheese sandwich. Mom's specialty. A lump catches in my throat when I remember Mom's tear-streaked face at dinner last night.

I need to pull out all the stops today when I show Mom and Dad my room. Nothing halfway. Everything depends on how they feel when I open that door.

I grab a sheet of notebook paper from my desk and sketch a map of my room while I eat.

What will impress Mom and Dad the most about me? Obviously, I can't highlight my elite gamer abilities, since I'm grounded and all. I mean, I have plenty of GamerCon posters that tell that story. There are plenty of other screen-free things I could show them too.

I'm pretty sure they know I love science and reading. But they might have forgotten how many science fairs I've won (with Evan and Q, of course). Better make sure all my science fair medals are hanging up.

They know I love Zip, so they know I love animals. But maybe I could remind them that I love nature, especially growing things.

This time, though, I'll put my Lego builds up higher. So Mom doesn't crush them (again). If she steps on my marshmallow tower, that's no big deal. I ought to move my race car battle zone out of the way, though.

I'm putting the finishing touches on my sketch when the classroom door opens, the lights blink on and Mrs. Peddy yelps.

"Jeff! Why are you sitting here in the dark? Are you all right?"

"Um, hi. Yeah." I fold my map into quarters and shove it into my pocket. "I'm fine. Everything's fine." I smush my paper lunch bag into a ball and dart to the trash bin in three awkward leaps.

She tucks her purse into a cubby under her desk, sits

in her cushiony chair, and flips open her laptop. "We miss you at Science Club."

My cheeks feel like hot sandbags. "Thanks. How's our project going?" I hope my voice sounds more enthusiastic from the outside, because from the inside it sounds saggy.

"Let me see." She plucks a pen from behind her ear. "If I remember correctly, Nicole and Vincent handed in your proposal revisions last week."

Nic and Vince? Since when is Vince in Science Club? And why is he working on my/our project? "What happened to Evan and Q?" I scour my desk with a wet paper towel.

"Evan and Quenton chose a less scientifically rigorous project." She points to a table in the corner. A sad-looking pile of papier-mache sits on a plastic mat.

"Is that... a baking soda volcano?"

Mrs. P smiles like she's sharing a secret. "I think it will be, if they choose to finish it."

Seriously? Baking soda volcanos? Come on. We made those by accident a couple of weeks ago. That's hardly a challenge. It's like Evan and Q don't even take science seriously anymore.

"How about your research? Are you still working on your book?" Of course, Mrs. P remembers.

I smile. "Yeah."

"Do you have it with you? May I see it?"

"Sure," I say. I lift my masterpiece out of my backpack and present it to her. She flips through the first pages, then slowly scans the latest chapters. "What kind of work does your mom do?"

"She works for a real estate agency."

"Ah." Another quiet minute passes while she reads, then she closes the notebook. "You've made a lot of progress since the last time I saw this, haven't you?"

It doesn't feel like it. "Sort of. I think I'm learning. But I don't know if it's progress. I'm still grounded."

Mrs. P passes my book back. "Have you shared this with anyone besides me? Any friends? Mom and Dad?"

"Just my sister Sadie. And you. I was going to tell Evan and Q about my experiment today at lunch, but they're not here. If anybody else wants to read it, they can buy a copy."

Mrs. P laughs. "Fair enough. I'm honored to review an advance copy." She leans in and her smile fizzles a little. "But I think your parents ought to get a preview too. You should ask them to read what you've written."

I squint at Mrs. P. "Why?"

"There's a scientific principle called Occam's Razor. Do you know it?"

"No."

"Occam's Razor says that when faced with multiple explanations, the simplest one is usually the most likely. Letting your parents know how you feel—by inviting them to read your book—might be the simplest path to regaining some freedom," she says. "Just a thought."

The door opens. I nod my thanks and return to my seat as my classmates flood the room.

I was planning to tell Evan and Q about my experiment. Why couldn't I share the whole book with Evan and Q? They might actually think it's cool. You know, since it's scientific and everything.

But asking Mom and Dad? That's not happening. You know that expression, 'he's an open book?' I'm pretty sure whoever said that was talking about me. I mean, I tell my parents how I feel All. The. Time. They know I want to hang out with my friends and go to GamerCon. How could they not? They don't need to read my book to know this about me.

No offense to Mrs. P, but she doesn't know my parents the way I do. If my parents read one word of my book, I'd never get ungrounded. Like, ever.

Plus, they'd take red pens and rewrite everything. Actually, no. They'd get the shredder out and rip it to pieces. Then they'd set it on fire in the fire pit (that I made, by the way).

If the scenes in my head are anything close to what might actually happen?

Sorry, Mrs. P. There's no way I'm letting them near that notebook.

Chapter 21

Guess who was actually at school today? Evan and Q. How do I know this? They're standing together in the bus line after school. I'm half stunned, half super-pumped to see them, so I practically run up to where they're standing. "Hey! Where were you at lunch today? I looked for you."

Evan pulls out his phone and says nothing.

Q raises his chin and says "Evan's mom took us out to lunch. We would have asked you, but you probably couldn't have gone anyways. You ungrounded yet?"

Q might as well have kicked me in the gut. They went out to lunch. Them. They didn't even bother to ask me. Because of my parents.

"Not yet. Getting closer though. Today might be the day."

Evan snort-laughs. "Oh man. You're kidding, right?"

"Um. I hate to tell you, but GamerCon is three days away." Q shoves his hands in his pockets. "You're not going, dude. As long as your mom and dad are fighting, they're going to be—"

"Fighting? With me? We don't fight. They just ground me and that's it." I want to tell him how I'm about to get un-grounded, but Q is quick to jump back in.

"No, not with you, dude," Q says. "I didn't want to say anything, but you should know. Sometimes we hear them yelling. Like, from across the street. My parents think your parents are headed for divorce."

"Divorce? No way. They might have yelled a couple times. At me, not each other. They're just... always in a bad mood, so they sound like they're fighting. But they're not." I glare. Q sits in his awkward wrongness for a second. "They're *not*."

"Okay okay." Q holds his palms facing forward in the classic 'I surrender' pose. "If you say so."

"I say so." *How can Q even think that? My parents aren't getting a divorce.*

Are they?

"Anyway," Q says. "Why don't you just lay low for a bit? Chill. Things will blow over."

"Blow over? Right. Have you met my parents? It'll blow over like a hurricane."

"You're killing me," Evan says.

I ignore him and keep talking to Q. "I *have* to do something. If I don't, I'm gonna miss out on everything. I already missed out on your sleepover, and lunch today."

Evan shoves his phone in his pocket, squares his shoulders with mine, and—finally—looks me right in the eyes. "You know what you *have* to do? You have to shut up. We'll bring you a t-shirt from GamerCon, okay? Shut. Up. Everybody gets in trouble sometimes. Quit whining about it and deal with it."

I feel like I just took a dodgeball smack in the face. I don't like it. I don't like getting left behind. I don't like being told the Maxwells can hear my parents fight across the street. My hands clench into fists. My body feels like one of those stupid baking soda volcanos right before the foam starts flying. "Who are you telling to shut up?"

Quenton steps between us. "He's just saying that it's time for you to take the punishment and move on. You're trying too hard."

Why do my best friends want me to admit defeat? It's like they don't care about GamerCon at all. "Are you kidding me? No way. We've been talking about this for months. I'm not giving up on you guys. I have a plan. It's awesome. Totally failproof. We're going to GamerCon together. We have to. Don't we?"

My question floats in the air like an empty fishhook in the water. I cross my arms and wait for their response.

"Of course we do." Q claps a hand on my shoulder. "I hope your plan works."

Evan sighs. "Yeah. Me too. But look, man. If you can't go, you can't go. It's not that big a deal."

The school bus rumbles up to the curb and Evan walks to the carpool line to wait for his mom. The bus door scrapes and squeals open and kids pile in. Q and I shuffle aboard and drop into our usual seats.

He spends the whole bus ride texting. Probably with Evan. I'm still grounded from my phone, of course. So I'm left out again.

It's not that big a deal, Evan says. Hanging out at GamerCon is all we talked about for weeks and now it's *not that big a deal?*

And Q? He thinks my parents are getting a divorce. That's the dumbest thing I've ever heard. He says I should chill? Well, *I* think my *Mom and Dad* should chill, and let me hang out with my friends.

It won't be long now. Today's lunch? It's the last time Evan and Q leave me behind.

I can feel it.

Chapter 22

By the time I climb off the bus, I am ready to get to work. Which is good, because I have less than an hour to prepare my room for Mom and Dad.

So what if Evan and Q want me to give up. That's okay. We don't have to agree on everything. But for real—they're super wrong and I know this will totally work. This is a no-fail plan. It has to be, if I want to get ungrounded and keep my best friends.

I barrel down the hall to my room.

If there was ever a kid whose room deserved its own reality tv series, it's me. I ought to know. I spend a ton of time in there, what with being grounded all the time.

My room is pure awesomeness. And now I'm about to share this awesomeness with my parents. So, everything has to be perfect.

First things first. I put my Lego model of the Empire State Building on top of my bookshelf. For safety.

I re-stack my laundry sculptures on the corner of my bed. Are they fluffy and lifelike? Check.

I close the curtains, so the late afternoon sunlight doesn't frizzle my ant farm. Nobody wants to look at a farm full of dead ants.

Next, I hop, leap, and skip through my sockstacle course to make sure it's parent ready. Mom's totally going to love this. It's the next best thing to PE. Or, in her case, Zumba class.

The last thing is music. Do I need background music? I pull Dad's vintage tape recorder out from beneath my bed. This will have to do.

Where's the map I drew at lunch? Oh yeah. I pull it out of my pocket and review.

Entrance and exit—conveniently located in one place—check

GamerCon posters—obviously—check

Bookcase—because I love reading—check

Laboratory— where my science fair medals are —check

Marshmallow tower—building stuff is awesome—check

Writing desk—where *haiku* magic is made—check

Ant farm—nature is amazing—check

Sockstacle course—for physical fitness—check

Laundry sculptures—creativity and resourcefulness—check

Blanket fort/reading nook—everyone needs one—check

Big finale: Jeff's living closet—I grew this myself—

check.

I almost forgot. Invitations. I tear a sheet of paper from my notebook and scrawl

ONE DAY ONLY
Mom and Dad are cordially invited to
Tour de Jeff
Today, now, in Jeff's Room

I step back and absorb all my hard work. This is going to be perfect. I can't believe I didn't think of this sooner. It's like giving Mom and Dad a backstage tour of their favorite old-timer's rock band. Only better. Because it's exclusive, insider info about their very own son.

They love me, so they're going to love this.

The garage door gears grind and Zip barks his way to the kitchen door. I slide the invitation into my back pocket and butterflies in my belly flutter up to my throat.

Pipe down, butterflies. I know exactly what to do.

It's showtime.

Chapter 23

I open my door and stand with one foot in my room and the other in the hallway. Technically, I haven't left my room. Also technically, I have.

"Hey there, Zipparoo!" Dad's in a decent mood.

The only thing I hear from Mom is the thud of her purse on the counter.

Deep breath. My life is minutes away from being back to normal.

"Starting now—Tour de Jeff, Starring Jeff! Stop in for thrills! Chills! Fun for the whole family!" I yell down the hall in my best WWE voice. Okay, maybe I'm a little dramatic. I have to get their attention.

It works. On Sadie.

She opens her door and peeks across the hall. "Ooh! Is it time? Good luck!" She gives me two thumbs up.

I give her two thumbs up in return. "Thanks." She disappears into her room, leaving me to my work. Which I would totally do if Mom and Dad had responded at all to my WWE-style announcement. Better try again.

"Mom! Dad!" I yell. "Could you come here? Please?"

I stand outside my door, next to the NO PARENTS PAST THIS POINT sign. Am I smiling? Yes. Wide enough to show teeth, but not so wide that I look creepy.

The first thing I notice: Mom is definitely in Proceed With Extreme Caution. Dad's Somewhat Happy. It's a start.

With both hands, I present the invitation to Mom. She unfolds it and reads. Dad peeks over her shoulder.

"It's been a long time since I hung this sign on my door. But as an exclusive, special treat, for one day only, Mom and Dad? I invite you to enter... my room." I pull the blue painter's tape off the corners, and the NO PARENTS sign falls off my door.

Thunk.

"What is this?" Mom asks, looking at Dad. A corner of her mouth lifts. Did she just shift into Somewhat Happy? I knew it. I knew this would work.

"Welcome. Please enjoy this peek inside my world."

I stand back and hold my arm out, you know, in the international gesture of invitation.

They step inside my room like they're walking barefoot into a cow pasture.

I press "play" on the rickety tape player. A theme song from some old sci-fi TV show whines in the background. It's kind of eerie, but it will work.

"Let's take a tour, shall we?" I ask in my best game show host voice. "I've grown up a lot since the last time you were in here. Of course, I have the original Fire Ant

Hero poster and my collection of GamerCon posters on the walls. And here, you'll probably notice my bookcase has a few more books in it." I tug my copy of Dr. Seuss's "Oh, the Places You'll Go!" from its place on the shelf. "Remember this one, Mom?"

"Aw, that was your favorite book in kinder." Mom's eyes shine.

"I still love reading, you know." I hand her the book and motion us forward. "Right here's my lab." I slide my lab coat off its hook and slip it on over my t-shirt.

"Isn't this my old work bench?" Dad runs his hand along the edge of my lab table. "I thought the Salvation Army picked this up."

"I got to it first. It's my science lab now. Isn't it awesome? This is where Evan, Q, and I created projects that made science fair history. Check it out. We won every year since third grade." I point at the medals dangling from hooks along the wall.

Mom squints at the stack of gear stashed beneath the table beneath my chemistry set. "Is that a fire extinguisher?"

"Of course! There was an extra in the garage, so I borrowed it, you know, just in case." I say. "Lots more to see." I step forward, and they follow.

"What is happening right now?" Dad whispers.

It's amazing how good it feels to show Mom and Dad all the things I love. "On your left, you'll see Marshmallow Tower." I stop next to my masterpiece, which is precision-balanced on the floor next to my lab. "Remember that gingerbread house competition we watched before Christmas?"

"Oh yeah! Great show." Dad says.

"It kind of inspired me. So I made this. It took nine chopsticks, 167 regular-sized marshmallows, and 72 mini marshmallows. Well, there were 82, but I ate some during construction."

"Has that been in here since Christmas?" Mom asks.

"Yep. Isn't it cool?" I walk backward, directing Mom and Dad toward the window. "We're moving, we're moving, we're stopping." I raise one hand like a traffic cop, then kneel by the window, next to my ant farm. "Okay, here we are. You'll want to lean in a little closer for this one. This is my ant farm and feeding station."

"Feeding station?" Mom grips Dad's arm.

I open the tiny door on top of the plastic tube. "Yeah! Do you want to try it?" Mom shakes her head, so I break a veggie chip into tiny pieces, drop it into the opening, and attach the tube to the ant farm. Almost immediately, worker ants file through and swarm the chips. "They love veggie chips. Look at them go. See? Nature is amazing, isn't it? Hours of fun."

I stand and face the corner of my desk. Mom and Dad do too. "We're going to take a quick break here at my writing desk. You know I'm good at video games and science, but I'm also a poet. This is where I write."

Dad purses his lips and nods, like, *not too shabby, son,*

but he doesn't say anything. He doesn't have to. I know he's impressed.

Mom's covering her nose and mouth with her sleeve. "That smell. What is it?"

I sniff the air, but all I smell is the sweet aroma of me about to be ungrounded. "Not sure." I shrug. "Next is the world-famous Sockstacle Course." I turn and point at strategically-placed sock mounds on my floor.

"Ah. Socks. That's it." Mom nods.

"It doesn't look like much, but don't let that fool you. This is designed to test your physical fitness skill and your imagination at the same time. I'll show you how it's done, then you guys follow me."

I stand at the beginning of the course. "I'm a spy, and I was just caught downloading blueprints for a top-secret teleportation device! I must escape!" I figure-eight between the first two sock piles, jump over the third, and hop backward on one leg over the last four just to show off my skill. "See? It's easy. Here's the secret: There's no one right way to complete the Sockstacle Course." I tell them. "Your turn. Dad, you first. Ready? Set? Go!"

Dad closes his eyes. "I'm an NBA legend at the all-star game." He opens his eyes and grins. He air-dribbles over the first pile, fake passes, then hops on his left leg over the second.

"Go Dad!" I cheer.

He leaps over the next three, spins around a tall one, and pretends to slam dunk over the last pile. "How'd I do?

Did I win?"

"You totally won. That was awesome." I high-five him. "Mom? You're up."

She's holding her nose. "Okay. So it doesn't batter how I do this?" Her brows furrow.

"You can do it any way you want." I pat her shoulder.

"Add your own style, Mom. It's your moment to shine." Dad winks.

"Ready? Set? Go!" I shout.

"But they're dirty socks."

"Aw, boo!" Dad teases. "They're not going to bite you. Come on, Mal."

Mom steps over each sock pile like it's something Zip left in the backyard. If I had a whistle, like Coach Matt in P.E., I'd blow it loud right now. "No, maybe I didn't explain it right. You get a do-over. Imagine the socks are anything you want."

Mom shakes her head. "Let's keep going."

At least Dad gets it. I guess Mom's tired or something. "Okay. No problem. I think you'll like my laundry art better anyway."

"I'm sorry, what?" I think I was right. Mom sounds exhausted.

"Laundry art." I stand next to the foot of my bed, eye-to-eye (if they had eyes) with my three slightly fluffy statues. "I had, like, a *lot* of laundry in here. And one day I thought, 'hey, that pile of laundry looks kind of like me, Evan, and Q.' So I sculpted it and shaped it a little more, and bam! Here they are. Laundry art. They're pretty great, don't you think?"

Pause to receive a hearty round of applause.

Hear none.

No problem. People didn't appreciate Picasso all the time, either.

"Jeff, honey, I need to get dinner started." Mom's looking at her watch. "Is this the last stop on our tour?"

She looks somewhat happy. Is she ready to give me back my freedom? It's been going pretty good so far. But to be absolutely certain, I need to finish strong. Good thing I saved the coolest thing for last.

"We can skip the blanket fort, I guess, but there is one more thing I really want to show you. I think you're going to love this. I have to turn off the lights, though." I hustle over, switch off the overhead light and give my eyes a second to adjust. "Okay, it's right over here." I lead them to my closet. "I found this down by the creek in the park, and I wanted to see if I could grow it myself." I open the door and smile at the familiar green-yellow glow shining from my closet floor.

Mom is so impressed that she actually yelps and yanks the collar of her shirt over her nose and mouth. Everything is going exactly as I planned.

"Meet *panellus stipticus*. Glow-in-the-dark mushrooms. Aren't they awesome?" Like I don't already know. Nobody answers, so I guess they already know too.

I switch the light back on and cross my fingers. When

I turn around, they're still standing at my closet door, staring at the wondrous nature inside. The room is silent except for the teeny scritch-scritch of ants lugging veggie chip pieces through their plastic tunnel.

I recognize this feeling. I'm at the end of a boss battle. The armadillo is down to one percent health and I'm mashing every single button on the controller. My heart is thumping. Triumph is in my reach and a victory dance is brewing in my bones.

"Well, what do you think?"

Are they happy? Are they *beyond* happy? I am.

The first thing I'm going to do when I'm ungrounded? Text Q and Evan and invite them over. We're going to celebrate big time.

Why are they so quiet? They're probably overwhelmed with love. And maybe a little embarrassment for punishing me so much.

"That. . . that is something," Dad closes the closet door. I was right. He's overwhelmed. He and Mom turn to face me. I'm so excited I can't help but bounce on my toes.

"We need to talk about the condition of your room." Mom places her hands together, prayer style.

This is it! I'm about to be free. "Pretty impressive, isn't it?" I shove my laundry friends onto the floor and leap onto my bed.

"Not the word I would have chosen." She taps a fingernail on my writing desk.

"I was thinking more along the lines of 'mind-boggling,' actually," Dad says.

Ah, yes. Dad gets it. "Thanks, Dad." I brace myself for more praise.

"To be clear, that isn't a compliment." Mom crosses her arms.

She just witnessed her only son's amazingness. Why isn't she smiling? Mom locks eyes with me. Dad looks like he wants to say something. But a look is as far as he gets.

"I've never seen a room like this before."

Well, no. Nobody's ever seen a room as amazing as mine before.

"This is unacceptable."

Unacceptable? That can't be right. "You mean, awesome, right? It's unacceptable because it's so awesome."

She ignores my question and keeps right on talking. "Here's what you are going to do. You will get rid of the mushrooms. The ants and the marshmallows go in the trash. Put all your laundry in a hamper where it belongs and carry that hamper to the laundry room. Take down the blanket fort. And you will do all of this tonight."

I suddenly feel like I'm carrying the entire fifth grade's backpacks on my shoulders. There's a humongous weight draped over me, pulling me down. Tears fill my eyes.

"But Mom!" This is not what was supposed to happen.

"No buts."

"Mallory, can we talk about this privately please?" Dad asks in a low voice, like he's trying to hide his question from me.

"Are you under the impression this topic is up for debate? Because it's not."

"I'm not debating. I just want to talk." His words say "not debating" but his voice says "I will arm wrestle you for Jeff's ant farm."

"Must you question every single thing I say?" Mom has asked me this exact same thing before. I can't help but wonder if there's ever a right answer.

"Last time I checked, I was his parent too." Dad says.

"You might try acting like it." Mom stalks down the hall.

Dad inhales. Holds it. Exhales. "Do what your mother says." He doesn't make eye contact with me. He just leaves.

This is not the post-tour victory lap conversation I expected. Where are my hugs and congratulations? Where are the apologies for keeping me grounded for so long? Where's my ticket to GamerCon?

Maybe Q's right. Maybe my parents are fighting more than I wanted to admit.

Maybe it's worse than that. Maybe they're fighting because of me.

Unacceptable me.

I kick the marshmallow tower. Not super hard, but hard enough. It tumbles into a sticky heap. I pluck a mini-marshmallow out of the pile and drop it into the ants' plastic feeding station.

I thought dozens of ants would swarm it, but only one storms into the tube. He lugs the sugary-pillow-from-the-sky onto his tiny ant shoulders. Compared to him, the mini-marshmallow is a boulder. The ant staggers back and forth, but he's determined. He keeps moving forward.

At least the ant still has a shred of hope.

HOW TO RAISE HAPPY PARENTS
by JEFF PENNANT

CHAPTER FOUR

OBSERVATION SESSION: EXPERIMENT

Wednesday, 5:07 pm

HYPOTHESIS: When I give Mom and Dad a tour of my room, they will be reminded of my awesomeness, overwhelmed with happiness, and unground me immediately.

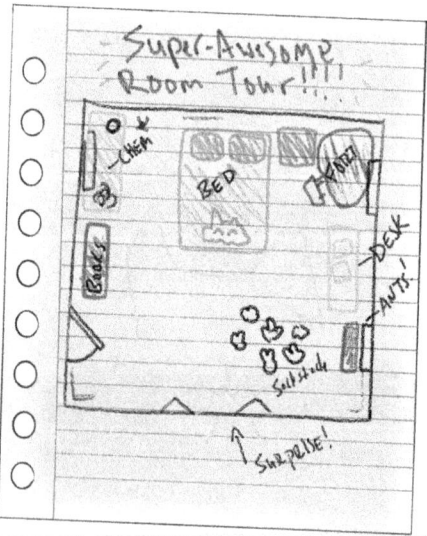

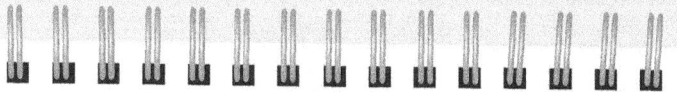

SUCCESS MEASUREMENT(s):

Visual Guide to Parental Happiness scale (both parents should be Full Happy)

Amount of yelling (should be zero)

Am I still grounded? (the answer should be no)

STATUS AT START OF EXPERIMENT:

Mom: Proceed With Extreme Caution

Dad: Somewhat Happy

Stop 1: Books: my love of reading

What they said: "I remember you liked Dr. Seuss in kinder"

First impressions: Off to a good start

Stop 2: Laboratory and Science Fair Medals: my scientific skills and winning track record

What they said: "Is that my work bench?" "Is that a fire extinguisher?"

First impressions: Still on track, they seem interested, asking questions

Stop 3: Marshmallow Tower: my ability to design and build

What they said: "liked the TV show," "has this been here since Christmas?"

First impressions: Seemed impressed but also seemed distracted by details

Stop 4: Ant Farm/Feeding Station: nature is cool and I love it

What they said: "Feeding station?"

First impressions: Maybe Mom and Dad were hungry?

Stop 5: Writing Desk/Poetry: fun fact about me

What they said: "What is that smell?"

First impressions: Mom has a sensitive nose

Stop 6: Sockstacle Course: fitness is more fun when you use your imagination

What they said: "NBA All-star," "But they're socks"

First impressions: Dad had fun, Mom may not like PE-type activities as much she used to

Stop 7: Laundry Art: I'm artsy and resourceful

What they said: nothing. Nothing at all.

First impressions: I thought they were too impressed with me to talk

Stop 8: *Panellus Stipticus*: Nature again, but with extra wow factor

What they said: More of a gaspy yelp than a word

First impressions: My first impressions were super wrong, but I thought they loved it and were about to let me go to GamerCon.

POST-TOUR:

What I expected: compliments, praise, immediate reversal of punishment

What they said: "Mind-boggling," "unacceptable."

What they did: They sentenced me to cleaning my room. Which means I had to get rid of almost everything cool about it.

INTERPRETATION OF FINDINGS:

This should have worked. I mean, at first they seemed happy. But by the end, they weren't. Why?

Once in a while, experiments go wrong. I'm not talking about a "whoops, I put dish soap in the beaker instead of baking soda" kind of wrong. I mean the "I used to have eyebrows before the explosion" kind of wrong.

In those experiments, if you're lucky, you grab a marker, draw your eyebrows back on, and learn from your mistakes.

Unfortunately, in this moment, I'm the eyebrow-missing scientist who doesn't have a marker.

Tour de Jeff should have worked. I shared the important stuff with them. Well, all the important stuff except video games and my friends, but they already knew that.

This was supposed to make them happy because it was about me.

Why didn't they like it? Don't they like me?

I think Dad did. His NBA-style sockstacle course moves were awesome. I think he was having a good time. Why didn't Mom?

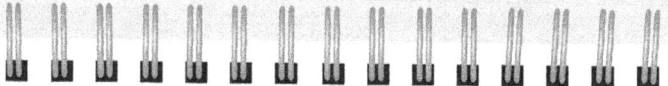

Parents are two different people, so it makes sense that they don't have the same exact point of view. But I think something was weird today. Mom and Dad are usually together on punishments. Even though he told me to do what Mom said, Dad didn't act like he was totally on board the Clean Your Room train.

I wonder if that's why I didn't get ungrounded. Maybe it's like my friend Q said. Maybe there's something wrong between Mom and Dad.

I think I need to re-evaluate my hypothesis. It's time to ask some new questions.

Am I grounded all the time because my mom is unhappy with my dad?

Are they getting a divorce?

If this is true, can I change it? How?

What kind of experiment would show me how they can be happy together again?

BONUS NOTES:

When a parent wants to "talk about the condition" of your room, it is most likely a trap. It's the kind of trap where you think you're going to get a compliment but you're really, really not.

Chapter 25

GamerCon is the day after tomorrow and I still can't go.

At school, I can't focus on my work. How do I face Evan and Q after my totally failproof experiment actually, you know, failed? By lunchtime, it feels like a swarm of mosquitos took over my insides. Everything buzzes and squirms.

Do I laugh it off and pretend it was all part of the plan? Should I tell Q, "Hey, you were right, my parents are fighting?"

What can I possibly say now?

But also, how do I *not* face Evan and Q? Even though things have been weird lately, they're still my best friends.

Why am I so worried? I mean, if things were different, if it were me and Q going to GamerCon and Evan was grounded and his parents were fighting, what would I do? If it were me, I'd do anything to help. I'd even ask my parents to talk to his parents.

Maybe I can ask Evan and Q to do that. They'd do that

for me, right? Or maybe I'll ask them to brainstorm with me. I'm sure together we can think of something I can do to make Mom and Dad happy enough to let me go. I can't believe I didn't think of this before. If anybody can help me, it's Evan and Q.

My mosquito-nerves have settled into a dull hum when I enter the cafeteria. I scan the room three times before I spot them at the center table, surrounded by the soccer-playing crowd. I smile. There's an empty seat next to Evan. He must have saved it for me.

I buy a cold milk and make my way over.

A kid in a Canada Reds soccer jersey is in the middle of a story when I sit. "You should have seen it. Evan totally flops—like, the most impressive flop of all flops you've ever seen. It was beautiful! The ref called it, too. Gave him the penalty kick. I couldn't believe it. You were brilliant, dude."

Why was Evan so brilliant? For flopping? What's a flop? Other than what my experiment did last night.

If I know Evan and Q, they're dying to know how last night went. When Canada Reds guy pauses his story to wolf down his cheeseburger, I jump right in. "You know my—"

"Dude, your slide tackle was even better. Like, none of their forwards could get past you." Evan reaches over and takes a couple of French fries off Canada's tray and pops them in his mouth.

He must not have heard me.

I lean behind Evan and tap Q's shoulder. "Q. Hey."

Q juts his chin toward me. "Hey." He leans forward

and chugs his Yoo-Hoo.

Then Canada Reds stands up. Evan, Q, and a couple of other guys do the same. They all take their trays and file out of the lunchroom. Q's empty Yoo-Hoo bottle is the only evidence that they were even here.

So that's it, then? No "Hey Jeff, how did it go last night?" No "Catch up with us after you're done eating and tell us how your plan worked." Just "Hey." They didn't forget, did they?

They probably didn't want to be rude to their soccer buddies is all. Best friends understand that kind of thing. I finish my sandwich and—carefully—hurry out of the lunchroom. But by the time I get outside, Evan and Q are in the middle of a soccer game. With Canada Reds dude.

I'm the only person standing on the sidelines, which is a little awkward. But fine. I have to get their attention somehow. Whenever they run past, I shout and wave and jump. "Guys! Hey!"

Soccer must be hard to play because they stay like, super focused on the ball. But I keep trying. And yeah, Trevor Wickham and his buddies ask me if I forgot my pom-poms because ha ha I look like a cheerleader. Whatever.

Finally, the teacher on duty blows the whistle and it's time to go inside. I run over to Q, but he and Evan are in the middle of a pack of sweaty soccer players. They're surrounded by a human moat, and I can't wade through it. I follow the group inside, thinking maybe I'll get a chance to at least say hi, but no. They don't even look in my direction.

Maybe after the crowd breaks up they'll come back for me.

I linger in the classroom doorway until Mrs. P ushers me into the room and closes the door.

Huh. Maybe not.

Chapter 26

The last bell rings and for the first time ever, I'm kind of dreading Science Club. Not *dread* dreading, because duh science, but not excited.

Maybe it won't be so bad. It can't possibly be as bad as lunch. I mean, I might actually get to talk with Evan and Q. Canada Reds guy and his soccer crew have never been to Science Club. So it has that going for it.

When I get back to Mrs. P's classroom, two people are already sitting at my table. My stomach sours. It's not Evan and Q. It's Nic and Vince.

"Jeff! I'm so glad you're here!" Nic practically tackles me in the doorway, takes me by the arm, and pulls me to the table.

"Yes! Dude, we need your brain." Vince holds up a clipboard.

"I'm kind of using it right now. But okay. What's up?" I keep my eyes on the door. Maybe Evan and Q are running late.

Nic shoves her backpack under the table to clear a seat

for me. "I hope you don't mind, but, um, we were kind of hoping to work on your gaming experiment."

They want to join our Science Club project?

"I don't know. That was really a me, Evan, and Q thing."

"Well, they asked me to help, remember? I drew the central nervous system diagram for you?"

I remember. That feels like forever ago. "Well, yeah."

"We actually went ahead and answered Mrs. P's questions and turned your paper back in." Vince passes me the clipboard. Sure enough, there's a Mrs. P-approved proposal and a supply closet pass.

They finished our proposal? Without us? The hair on the back of my neck tingles. "Did you talk to Evan and Q about it first?"

"Of course. We did that first." Nic sits next to me. "We asked them a couple weeks ago. They said yes. Then they kind of stopped showing up."

That can't be right. Evan and Q not coming to Science Club? I feel like I'm wearing clothes that are three sizes too small. Everything is uncomfortable. "They'll be back. Trust me."

"Well, until then, what do you think? Can we work together?" Nic asks.

This idea tumbles around my brain like a sock in the dryer. On one hand, this gaming experiment isn't going to conduct itself. And Evan and Q did ask Nic for help. It's a pretty big experiment. When they come back to Science

Club, there will still be plenty of work to go around. "I guess if they told you they're okay with it, it's fine with me."

Vince points to the proposal. "We didn't change anything in your hypothesis or your steps. Take a look. We did add a chart for collecting results, though. What do you think?"

A chart? I love charts. "Can I see it?"

Nic flips the paperwork over to reveal a basic spreadsheet taped to the clipboard. "What do you think about making a graphic out of this data when we're done?"

I have an idea. "What do you think about making the graphic look like a videogame controller, or a handheld screen? Could you guys do that?"

"Yeah, that'd be easy," Vince says. "We could try drawing it a couple of different ways. You can pick the one you think works best. If you want."

We spend the rest of Science Club talking, ironing out details about how and when to start the experiment. Before I know it, the bus monitor shows up and it's time to go.

Bus 10 is quieter than usual today. Probably because Q isn't here. I sit in the front row and imagine he's sitting next to me. In my head, our conversation goes like this:

Me: I can't believe you guys didn't come to Science Club today. Where were you?

Q: I went to the dentist. You know I wouldn't miss Science Club if I didn't have to.

Me: You totally wouldn't.

Q: How did it go with your parents yesterday? Are you coming to GamerCon with us?

Me: It was a giant fail. I don't know what to do next.

Q: If you can't go, I won't go either.

Me: No, don't do that. But maybe ask your mom to call my mom? If your mom says it's okay, my mom might listen.

Q: You got it.

I hop off the bus and sit on my front porch. Maybe imaginary me is right—maybe Q did have a dentist appointment after school. Maybe he's on his way home right now. Wouldn't hurt me to wait a little while, so I can ask him to help me. Who knows? Maybe Evan is with him, and I can talk to them both. I can totally feed two birds with one seed, or whatever that expression is.

The grumble of a car approaching pops my thought bubble. Is it Mrs. Maxwell's car? Are Q and Evan with her? I hop to my feet and bounce. *Please please please let it be them.*

A boxy brown car rolls around the corner and the garage door churns open. Suddenly my legs are made of lead. No more bouncing. It's Dad.

How long have I been sitting here? Is it really time for Dad to be home from work already? How come he's home before Mom?

My instinct is to make a run for my room, but there's no point. Dad's already seen me. Judging by his Steer Clear expression, he's not happy to find me on the front porch, either.

Dad stands in front of me at the bottom of the porch steps. "You look like you've had a lousy day. Everything ok?"

Is everything okay? Aside from losing my best friends because of him and Mom? "Everything's fine."

He reaches up, grips my backpack by a shoulder strap, and lugs it over his shoulder. "Let's go inside. Mom had an appointment after work so I'm cooking dinner tonight. Maybe you can share your spaghetti recipe, eh?" Zip barks from his sentry post in the living room. "Come on. Zip's waiting."

I steal a last look across the road at Q's empty driveway, then head into the garage. "Is Mom okay? Is she sick or something?"

"Oh, no, nothing like that. She's fine. She just had some business to take care of." Dad pats Zip and kicks his work shoes into the hall closet.

Business? Talking-to-a-divorce-lawyer type of business? Or the regular kind, like going to the bank or the dry cleaners or something? "What kind of business?"

Dad hands me my backpack. "Don't you have homework? Or some chores to do?" He doesn't sound mad, exactly. But he sure doesn't sound like Dad either.

Chapter 27

I have one more day. That's it. If I'm going to have a shot at going to GamerCon tomorrow, I need Evan and Q's help. Or at least their parents' help. So when lunchtime rolls around, I hurry to our table. I have to talk to them before their soccer buddies get there.

I'm almost to the table, about to pull out a chair. Then there's a whoosh and a blur and I'm staring at a purple kitten ear headband. The kind that has a matching pair of leggings and is attached to Nic and is standing next to Vince.

They totally stepped in between me and my table. If I were the Hulk, I'd be ragey-green right now. But I'm not, so I take a deep breath. "Um, hey, I was about to sit there."

"You want to sit with us instead? We're right over there." She hitches her thumb toward the corner table where two other kids sit. "Do you know Addison and Kaley?"

"No, don't think so." I slide between them and put both hands on the back of the chair. That's the This Seat is

Mine move. It usually works.

Vince chugs a chocolate milk and stuffs the empty bottle in his hoodie pocket. "They're more into First Winter than Fire Ant Heroes, but they're still cool. You should meet them."

Other kids fill in at the table around us. *I can't lose my spot because of Nic and Vince.* "Why don't you two sit with me and Evan and Q today?" I motion toward the empty chairs. They don't budge.

"No thanks." Nic crosses her arms. "I don't know why you want to sit with them. They're not very nice to you."

My face stings, like she just yanked out my eyebrows. "What are you talking about? We're best buds. We joke around."

"No, *you* joke around. *You're* funny. *They* make fun of you. They're not funny, they're mean." She points a glittery-fingernailed index finger at me. "You need to decide what kind of person you want to be friends with." She turns and walks toward the corner table. Vince, of course, is right behind her.

I drop into my chair. What does she mean they make fun of me? Nobody makes fun of me. Well, besides Trevor Wickham. And that guy on the bus who said I smell like lasagna. He wasn't wrong though.

Just because we had a decent time at Science Club once doesn't mean we're best friends. It definitely doesn't mean she gets to tell me who to be friends with.

What do Nic and Vince know about anything, anyway?

I mean, their idea of being a good friend is what, accidentally being there when someone slips on a noodle? Randomly showing up at their house uninvited? Taking over their Science Club project? That's just rude, that's what that is.

I feel like my insides have an itchy rash I can't scratch. I'm so irritated that I've almost picked all the crust off my sandwich.

Q sits next to me. "Hey." He lays a paper napkin on top of his pizza slice. We watch the grease soak in and leave a dark orange blotch across the paper.

I've been waiting for my chance to talk with him. But now that he's here? I have so many things to say I have no idea where to start.

Thinking about it all makes me feel like I'm staring at the pieces of my go-kart in the driveway again. Or a bazillion-piece jigsaw puzzle. It's overwhelming. There are so many parts. I have no clue how to put it together.

"You were right." I almost choke on the words.

"Of course I was right," Q says. "About what?"

"My parents. Fighting. I think my mom met with a lawyer yesterday. Dad was acting all weird."

"Oh, man." He folds his less-greasy pepperoni slice in half. "Tough break, dude."

Evan kicks my shoe under the table as he sits down across from me. I usually hate when he does that. But today I'm so happy to see him I don't even care. He fist bumps Q across the table. "You ready for GamerCon tomorrow, Q? It's going to be epic."

Finally, the three of us are together again. Everything is going to be okay. "Guys. I need to ask you someth—"

Q pulls out his phone and they huddle around it. They whisper to each other.

"Um. Guys?"

Fun fact—phones aren't allowed in the cafeteria. Evan Graham and Quenton Maxwell are totally breaking school rules right now. They're not rule-breakers. Also, they're not paying any attention to me.

I yank the collar of my suddenly too-tight shirt. It's a thousand degrees in the cafeteria. If they get caught, it's an automatic lunch detention. If my parents ground me for forgetting chores, imagine how long I'll be grounded for getting detention.

"Guys! You're gonna get caught."

"Shush," Q hisses. "Saying it out loud might make it happen." He and Evan hunker over the table like they're trying to blend into today's taco salad. I keep an eye on the lunch monitor and his whistle as they weave through the aisles.

What is Q talking about? Saying something out loud makes it happen? That's ridiculous. If that were true, like, at all, people would go around saying stuff like 'I'm a superhero millionaire,' or 'I'm an Olympic medalist' and boom. The world would be full of superhero millionaire medalists.

Obviously, that's not happening.

But still, I wonder.

I want to go to GamerCon with my best friends. Could

it really happen if I say it out loud? I mean, I don't want to lie. Lying is the total opposite of factual accuracy.

But—is saying something that *isn't true yet* a lie? If something's not true yet, could saying it out loud *make* it true? That's not totally lying, is it? It's more like wishing out loud, right?

The two of them whisper and scroll over and over like I'm not here.

I'm like one of those background beetles in FAH3. I'm in the scene, but not important to the game.

I want back in the game.

Is lying my way back in?

If it's the way back to my friends, it's worth a shot. "I can go."

My mouth feels moldy and sour, like I chugged spoiled milk. I may throw up.

The whispering stops. Evan slides his phone into his back pocket and scoots back into his seat. He looks at Q, then at me. "You can go? To GamerCon?"

"I can." It's easier the second time, but I half expect a boulder to fall out of the sky and land on my head. It doesn't, but the feeling that *it might* settles into the back of my brain.

"Does this mean what I think it means? Your plan worked?" Q's eyes are wide, like he just saw a banana sprout from my forehead.

"That's um, one way of looking at it, yeah."

"That's great," Q says.

"Yeah. So great." Evan says to the ceiling.

"So, what time are we going? Can I catch a ride with you?"

"Well, I would say you could," Q speaks in his extra-polite voice. "But I'm staying over at Evan's tonight and riding with him tomorrow. Sorry." He glances at Evan.

"My sister and her friends are going too," Evan says. "Maybe we can meet up someplace early?"

On the outside, I'm sitting at the lunch table. Inside? I'm victory dancing like a boss. "Yeah! What about the ticket office? Would you guys want to meet there?"

"That would work," Q says. "Then we can go straight to the tournament."

"Sure." Evan stands and collects his and Q's lunch trays. "We can do that."

I leap to my feet and walk between Evan and Q to the trash bin. "Have you guys signed up for the tournaments already, or should we decide what we're doing when we get there? Maybe we should go—"

"We can figure it out tomorrow morning, right?" Evan opens the big double doors that lead to the schoolyard.

The three of us mosey out to the soccer field together. We form our own huddle on the sidelines, planning our tournament strategy. All three of us in the game together. Nobody left in the background.

Just like it used to be.

Chapter 28

I'm practically floating to the bus line after school when Mrs. P and her rolling backpack full of file folders stop me in the hallway.

"Aren't you forgetting something?" She smiles in that 'I know something you don't' way. "Your backpack?"

I do a quick self-inventory. Shirt. Pants. Socks. Shoes. *Whoops.* She's right. No backpack.

"Ugh. Thanks, Mrs. P."

"Are you forgetting something else?"

Something else? What is she talking about?

Wait. No way.

I think my heart just freaked out and fled my rib cage.

She doesn't know that I lied, does she? How would Mrs. P know that? I mean, she's super smart, but she's not a mind reader. Unless... Was she in the cafeteria? "Not that I know of. . . ." My earlobes pulse.

"You were going to update me on your experiment's progress? The one you were writing about?"

I exhale long and loud. "Oh, right. Sorry. It's going

kind of... slow."

She adjusts the thick purse strap on her shoulder. "Did you ever share your book with your parents?"

I cringe a little. If they didn't like my room, they *really* won't like my book. "No."

She makes a clucking sound with her tongue. "What a shame. I still believe that would speed your results quite a bit. Think about it, won't you?" She lugs her gear toward the teacher parking lot. "Have a great weekend."

I turn around and hustle to the classroom so I can grab my backpack before the student teacher leaves. I'm glad Mrs. P noticed I didn't have it. I'm really glad she didn't know about my lie. But now that sour flavor is in my mouth again. I think it's called Lying Liar. Man, that lingers worse than Nurse Traci's sour cream and onion breath.

Evan and Q pass by on their walk to the carpool line. "Ticket window—tomorrow morning!" Evan shouts.

"See you!" Q waves.

"Tomorrow morning! See ya!" I wave back.

What's that weird, stretchy feeling on the front of my face? Oh yeah. It's a smile. All the spoiled milk sour feeling in the world will be worth it to have Evan and Q back in our friendly groove again.

So how am I going to get Mom and Dad to take me to the convention center ticket window tomorrow morning?

The Pennant Parent Fortress is more fortified than ever. And my armor is down to like, nothing. No percent. If I don't show up tomorrow, Evan and Q will know I lied.

Lying to my friends is bad enough. But I did it once and it worked. Could I lie to my parents too? What would I even say? My stomach lurches just thinking about it.

I stand in the hallway, adjusting my backpack, and then I notice. It's empty. The hallway, not my backpack.

Which makes me think I've missed the bus.

I walk outside to check.

Confirmed. I've missed the bus.

Great. I can't exactly call for a ride without my cell phone. And Sadie's already left for dance class with Mrs. St. John.

So, what, I'm supposed to wait until my parents get home from work and figure out I'm not home yet? That won't end well. I can't ask Mom and Dad to take me to GamerCon if I'm sitting on the curb at school. Also, missing the bus doesn't exactly send the "I'm a responsible kid" type of message I want.

But walking home on my own? Solving my own problem? That ought to do it.

I'll just have to walk home.

Me, my backpack, and I walk to the corner and head down Elkhorn Street. While I walk, I practice asking Mom and Dad if I can meet Evan and Q at GamerCon.

Me: Mom? Dad? Can I meet Evan and Q at GamerCon tomorrow morning? Please?

Mom/Dad: You know you're grounded, mister.

Me: Please? It's important.

Mom/Dad: Go to your room.

I even pretend I'm Mom and Dad and send myself to my room, so it's super realistic. Too realistic. No matter how I phrase it, the end result is always N-O.

Maybe if I take a different approach? Not lying, but not exactly truthful either?

Me: The Fire Ant Heroes tournament is tomorrow at GamerCon. It's too late for us to back out. Can you take me to GamerCon in the morning?
Mom/Dad: Hmm. Maybe.

I'll take a maybe. But I get the sour-milk-burps just thinking about lying again. Grammy used to say God uses all kinds of ways to nudge us toward doing the right thing. I wonder if that incudes sour-milk-burps. I also wonder what Grammy would say if she knew I lied. A tangy, spoiled flavor floods my mouth, and I know the answer.

Now, I'm at the neighborhood park. It's just six blocks from my house. I'm practically home already.

Why do I ride the bus, anyway? This walking thing isn't so bad. There's fresh air, sunshine, a creek, and hey—a turtle!

A tiny turtle, probably the size of my fist, is clawing his way along the creek bank. I pick him up. His legs swipe back and forth, like scaly windshield wipers with claws. "Hey, little fella. Are you all alone out here?

Turns out, he isn't. There's another one. This guy isn't much bigger than the first one. But he's launching, like, the world's slowest attack against my tennis shoes. "You two know each other?"

I kneel and set them together, turtle face to turtle face. One turtle retreats into its shell and looks like a big green rock. The other one—the one who isn't an Adidas fan—it doesn't retreat at all. It stretches its neck way out, and I see something cool. It has bright yellow rings around its eyes. Kind of like Q's glasses.

"I shall name you Quenton." I tap it gently, then nod toward the one pretending to be a rock. "You shall be Evan."

"Guys. I did something stupid." Turtle Q looks up at me. "Yeah. I did. I lied to you. Well, the people versions of you. Those guys are my best friends and I lied."

I know they're only turtles. But still. I feel five pounds lighter after I say the truth out loud. This feels way better than sour milk burps. Grammy was right.

I slide them into my backpack and leave the zipper open. For breathing. Then I walk the rest of the way home.

Mom's gardening tools are on the front porch. I borrow them and fill one of her buckets with dirt and rocks from the front flowerbed. I haul the bucket and my backpack to the bathroom I share with Sadie. Zip follows me close. I think he likes turtles.

It takes me no time at all to create a perfect turtle habitat in the bathtub. I use rocks and dirt to make a turtle-sized island at one end. In the deeper end by the drain? It's a swimming hole. And it's awesome.

Q likes to hang out at the shallow end of the tub. Evan prefers swimming in circles and trying to claw his way out. Kind of like me, trying to figure out how to ask Mom and Dad to let me go to GamerCon tomorrow morning. Makes me dizzy just thinking about it.

"You probably want to know what I lied about. Okay. I told them I was allowed to go someplace with them that I can't."

Turtle Evan digs deep into the mud. Turtle Q blinks. I can't tell if it's a judge-y blink or just a regular blink.

"It gets worse, though. Here's the thing. If I don't go with my friends, I don't think they're going to be my friends anymore. They're the only friends I have. So do I tell my parents that I lied? Or do I lie to them too?"

Dad always says it's important to be factually accurate. Lying is the opposite of that. Maybe that's why my head is all spinny and my breath smells like moldy cheese.

If I lie to my parents? I might get to go to GamerCon. But it will be another layer of lie.

I don't want to be that guy.

I'll tell Mom and Dad the truth. I'll tell them what I said to Evan and Q today. And I'll ask them if I could please go. They haven't been proud of me for much, but maybe they'll be proud of me for admitting I messed up.

"Thanks for listening, guys. You're good friends." Q scrapes a tiny claw through mud and stares at the bathtub wall. Evan pretends to be a rock again. I don't know why I expect turtles to have answers.

But I do know this. If I don't make it to GamerCon tomorrow and I lose the real Evan and the real Q, these guys are the next best thing.

Chapter 29

If I want Mom and Dad to say "yes," I need them to be at least Somewhat Happy. And let's face it. If I knew how to make them happy, I wouldn't be in the situation I'm in right now.

But I have to try. And I can't do it halfway.

In the past, what have I done to get in trouble? Let's see. There's skipping my chores. Gaming after school. Having friends over without permission. Building a fire. I haven't done any of those things in weeks.

What did they want me to do instead?

Have zero fun—got that one down. No friends over. Already done.

Chores.

If it means I get a chance to hang with Evan and Q? Okay, fine. I'm in.

I take out the trash. I empty the dishwasher. I put the clean dishes away in their actual right places. I go to my room and practice my "I Messed Up and Lied to My Friends and May I Go to GamerCon Please Oh Please" speech in front of the mirror probably a hundred times.

By the time Mom and Dad get home from work, the sour milk taste in my mouth is gone. But I'm more nervous than a third grader before their first Science Fair.

They're in the kitchen, talking. I can't fully identify their happiness level from their voices. I need intel. A tiny peek ought to do it, but is it worth the risk of getting caught? Better to find out now than to be surprised later. I tiptoe down the hall and peer around the corner into the kitchen.

Eyebrows level. No frowns. No smiles. Proceed With Extreme Caution.

"Jeff?" Mom spots me and I freeze.

Nothing halfway.

"Can I help with dinner?" I step into the kitchen.

Mom and Dad look at each other like they weren't sure they heard me correctly. Dad nods and smiles. "That's the best question anyone's asked me all day."

"Thank you for the offer." Mom walks over and wraps me in a hug. "You can set the table, please." She smiles.

And there it is. Somewhat Happy achievement unlocked.

I work my way around the table, putting everything in place. Mom hums while she chops veggies for a salad. I take a deep breath.

Is now the best time to ask? Or should I wait until after dinner?

"Mal, you'll know this one." Dad stirs onions, peppers,

and chicken in a frying pan at the stove. "What's a sea monster's favorite meal?"

"Chicken of the Sea?" Mom asks. "No. Tuna salad?"

"Nope. Fish and ships." I groan and they laugh a little too long.

I think I'd better wait.

Our kitchen bustles like Queen Adlee's anthill in FAH3. When I offer to stir the chicken for Dad so he can change out of his work clothes, he high-fives me. Mom tries to throw carrot slices into my mouth from across the kitchen. She's almost being cool. I'm actually a little sad we have to stop when it's time to eat.

Afterward, Sadie goes to get ready for her sleepover at Avery's. I clear the table and head back to my room.

It's now or never.

I'll start with the truth—that I lied to Evan and Q about being able to go to GamerCon. Then I'll ask if they'll let me go. Maybe they'll have some sympathy for me. Maybe they won't. But at least I won't pile lies on top of lies until I'm Lying Liar, Mayor of Liartown.

I stand up tall and open my door. "Mom? Dad? Can you come in here for a minute?"

That's when we hear Sadie.

I'm pretty sure everyone on the planet hears Sadie. Her shrieks are like a wounded werecat. Like six wounded werecats. In a tunnel made of marble.

"Whyyyyyyy?" She bursts into my room, bawling and storming straight at me, fists clenched.

I back away from her until I wham into my closet door. "What is wrong with you?"

Sadie's sobbing and trying to talk at the same time. "You... know... I'm... scared... of... TURTLES."

She can't be serious. I've never heard her say this. Ever.

"Is this a joke? Since when?"

I'm not totally sure what Sadie says in response, because it sounds like wailing hiccups.

"Does she look like she's joking?" Mom gathers Sadie into her arms and glares. "What did you do?"

I can't answer that question because Sadie's horrible sireny crying sounds again. I don't know what she's trying to say. I just know she's miserable. As best I can tell, she either had a bad show-and-tell experience in first grade, or someone named Shawndel brought an evil pet turtle to a play date. Turtles left a terrible impression on her.

And I made two of them a home in our bathtub.

Oh man. I feel smaller than a fire ant at the base of a mountain.

"Sadie, I'm sorry. I had no idea. Really. I didn't know."

Zip races past, barking up a storm. The doorbell rings. The four of us freeze. Well, we all freeze except Sadie. She's still going strong.

"What now?" Mom ushers the screeching, red-faced mucus bubble that used to be my sister across the hall into her bedroom.

"Jeff, get the door, please." Dad follows Mom into Sadie's room, clutching a box of tissue in each hand.

I peek through the peephole and shudder. It's Mrs. Fischer. Judging by the frowny eyebrow angle, we're one step away from another neighborly call to the authorities.

I open the door wide enough that she can see I'm alive, but not so wide that she can see all of Sadie's crazy. I'm a good brother that way.

"Hey Mrs. Fischer." I park my body in the gap like a barricade. Flash my most charming, Nothing-to-See-Here smile.

"Are your parents home?" She stares over my head into the house.

"They're with Sadie." Sadie wails behind me.

"I thought I heard screams." Mrs. Fischer rises slowly on her tiptoes. "All the way in my backyard. Is everything okay?"

"Yes, thanks. It's a brother-sister thing. You know how that goes." I force a chuckle, but she doesn't join in. "No fire. It's fine. Everything's fine."

I grab the doorknob and tug the door. Mrs. Fischer wedges her gardening-booted foot between the door and the frame. "I think I'd better talk to your mom and dad. Will you get them for me, please?" Her eyes lock with mine. She's more stubborn than the boss armadillo's dung beetle sidekick.

"I promise they're home. They're with Sadie."

"Jeff! Get in here NOW!" Mom yells.

I shrug. "So sorry, I gotta go."

Mrs. Fischer pulls her foot away. "Tell your mother to

call me."

I yank the door closed.

For a second, I wonder if Mrs. Fischer is going to go home and call the police. When Mom yells "I SAID NOW!" I leave my wondering at the door and bolt to Sadie's room.

She's quieter now, but still crying. She sits, slumped over, on the edge of her bed. Mom stands next to her and presses a wet washcloth against the back of her neck. Dad sets an empty tissue box on her night table and walks toward me.

Do they think I did this on purpose? Once again, I'm about to get blamed for something that's not my fault. At least, something that I didn't mean to do, anyway.

"I swear I had no idea. I wasn't trying to—"

"Your sister has been through enough. Let's give her some privacy. We need to have a chat." Dad wraps an arm around me and walks me into the living room. Mom follows so close behind me I can hear her breathing.

"Fine, but—"

"Enough." Mom grips the back of Dad's recliner. "Why on earth would you traumatize your sister like that?"

I perch on the edge of the couch. "I didn't mean to. I promise. I had no idea turtles would upset her so bad."

"What in the world were you thinking?" Dad sits on the recliner across from me.

"I mean, you made me throw away my ant farm, so. . ."

"That's not an acceptable answer," Mom says. "Let's

start over. Where did all that dirt come from?"

"Where does anybody get dirt? From the ground. In the flowerbed."

What kind of question is that?

"Think about your tone when you talk to your mother." Dad uses a voice I've only heard him use with telemarketers. "I know you understand the question, so give her a real answer."

I thought I was giving her a real answer.

"Okay, okay, sorry. But come on. Everybody knows where dirt comes from."

"Jeff," Mom says through gritted teeth. "Why are there turtles in your bathtub?"

They want a real answer. A factually accurate, honest answer. What do I have left to lose? It will take a miracle for me to get to GamerCon tomorrow.

"I missed the bus, so I walked home. I saw the turtles at the park. I wanted to keep them, and I brought them home. I don't see what the big deal is. How was I supposed to know Sadie'd freak out?"

Mom presses her fists into the back of Dad's chair like she's propping herself up. "You walked home? By yourself?"

I nod.

Dad drops his chin to his chest.

See, this is the part where they should be proud of me for being self-sufficient. But instead? Mom asks more questions. "Why did you miss the bus? What happened?"

Why did I miss the bus? I missed the bus because I forgot

my backpack. I missed the bus because I was thinking about how miserable it felt to lie right to my friends' faces. I wanted us to be the same again. The unstoppable team. The bestest of best friends. And we're not now, not really. Because you and Dad don't stop grounding me. You don't see how hard I try to be a decent kid. No, not a decent kid. An awesome kid who wants to have fun with his friends. And now I'm about to lose all that. I'm about to lose everything. And you're worried about me missing the stupid bus.

"Son. I need you to focus." Dad leans forward. "Can you do that for me?"

I have nothing left to lose.

So why can't I tell them?

"Sure. I got distracted."

"I know."

"No, *I got* distracted. That's why I missed the bus."

It's factually accurate.

"And you didn't call us why, exactly?" Mom asks.

I turn my empty jeans pockets inside out. "You have my phone."

Also, factually accurate.

"No. You didn't have *your* phone. You could have used the phone in the office."

"I can use Mrs. McClanahan's cell phone?" I don't know the school secretary all that well. Why would I borrow her cell phone?

She raises her eyebrows. "Not her cell phone. The phone on Mrs. McClanahan's desk. The one that anyone can ask permission to use. Especially if they miss the bus and need to call their parents."

But calling my parents means talking with my parents. And talking with my parents lately? That means t-r-o-u-b-l-e.

"Walking home by yourself isn't a good idea. It's not safe," Dad says.

Mom nods. "You need to *think*, sweetheart."

I bolt to my feet. "I *do* think! I think 'Mom and Dad are going to be so mad that I missed the bus.' Then I think, 'hey, it's not that far, I can walk,' and then I think maybe—*maybe*—if I solve my own problem, I won't get in trouble. Again.' But no. I think wrong. You get mad anyway. You always get mad anyway. You're mad right now."

Factually. Accurate.

"I can't have this conversation right now," Mom says. "Please? You are wearing me out."

"I'm wearing *you* out?"

"Bottom line," Dad says, "you cannot keep a turtle in the house. You *absolutely* cannot keep a turtle in your bathtub. It scares your sister."

"*That's* the bottom line from today?" Mom walks around to the front of the recliner and faces Dad.

"Turtles," I correct them.

"What?" Mom and Dad glare at each other.

"Turtle-zzz. Turtles. Plural. You said I can't have *a* turtle. There are two. Factual accuracy is important."

"Yes, but. . . .Yes. But you still. You still can't. . . ," Dad stammers. He buries his face in his hands.

Mom sighs long and loud. "Your dad and I need a moment before the three of us talk about your consequences. Please go clean up the bathroom." She and Dad file out of the living room into the kitchen.

I'm down to zero energy. Zero health. Game over.

I'm calling it—I'm not going to GamerCon. I don't have best friends. I don't even have my turtle friends. Because they melted my big sister.

I skulk to the bathroom. Q lifts his tiny head when I turn on the light. His yellow-ringed eyes look haunted. Like, this turtle has seen way more than he ever thought he'd see in his lifetime. Evan claws at the corner. He's determined to scrape his way to freedom.

It's silly, I know, to be upset over a couple of turtles. They're not my pets. I found them a couple of hours ago. They're wild creatures. I know they're better off in the woods. And it's not like I don't already have the best dog ever, because I totally do.

For a little while, I had two new best friends. It wasn't much, but still. It hurts to have to give them up.

"I'm sorry fellas." I lift them from the tub and head down the hall.

Then I hear Mom and Dad talking in the kitchen.

Mom's voice is like an extra-short haircut. High and tight. "He's eleven years old. That's old enough to know how to use the office phone in an emergency. What if he had been kidnapped? Do you think we need to call Dr. Austin?"

"Are you serious, Mallory? You want to call the pediatrician because our kid is acting like a kid? You said it yourself. He's e-lev-en. I don't think we need to alert the medical community."

"Why do you always take his side?" Mom's volume dials up to 9/10.

"Okaaay." Dad engages his I'm-extra-calm-because-one-of-us-has-to-be protocol. "Number one, we're a family and we're all on the same side. Number two, having empathy for the kid doesn't mean I don't think consequences apply."

Mom lets loose an exaggerated sigh. I flatten my body ninja-style against the wall and inch my way closer. They are arguing again, that is clear.

Also clear? They're arguing about me.

"He's a kid. What kid doesn't get carried away sometimes?" Dad asks.

"What happens when he's in junior high? Or high school? What happens when he decides to do one of his chemistry experiments in his locker? Or he thinks maybe the homework isn't really due when the teacher says?"

"I think you're creating trouble where there isn't any."

"Am I? He doesn't seem to think he has to do what we ask—at least, not if he can explain his way out of it. When he gets caught, he ignores every consequence, or he tries to negotiate his way out."

I'm confused. I absolutely think I have to do what they ask. They're my parents. But why wouldn't I want a chance to explain myself? Mrs. P says in America we're all innocent until proven guilty.

"Every kid behaves this way once in a while," Dad says. "Some kids even manage to make money off it by recording it and putting it on YouTube. Maybe we ought to look into that."

There's a sniffing sound and I think Dad might be laughing at his own joke. It's tough to tell.

"It's not just once in a while, Matt. He's like this all the time. You've met kids who think the rules don't apply to them, haven't you? Those kids grow up expecting life to bend to their expectations. When it doesn't, they can't handle it. I don't want that for him."

I hear fingertips drumming on the kitchen table, then Dad says, "What do you want to do, ship him off to boarding school?"

I feel like when Dad says anything about shipping me off anywhere, Mom is supposed to laugh and say, "No, of course not. That's a ridiculous idea."

But she doesn't. There's a long stretch of silence.

"Do you think boarding school would help him? I can't be the enforcer all the time and you'd rather be his buddy than his dad."

"That's not true, and you know it," Dad's telemarketer voice says.

He says more, but I don't hear words. What I hear are two voices stuck on repeat in my head. "What do you want to do, ship him off to boarding school?" "Do you think it would help?" Over and over and over.

I can't believe what I just heard.

But I heard it.

They're sending me to boarding school.

My chest is tight as I tiptoe past the kitchen to the patio door. A big part of me wants to scream at them, like the way Sadie screamed when she saw turtles in the tub. The other part of me? It wishes I had a shell of my own I could hide in.

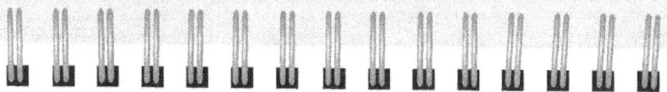

HOW TO RAISE HAPPY PARENTS
by JEFF PENNANT

CHAPTER FIVE

This will be my final chapter.

As I write this, at any moment, my parents might walk in, declare me unfit for our family, and ship me to boarding school.

Why do I think this? Evidence.

Tonight I observed Mom and Dad talking about me. Kind of. I overheard them talking. That's observing with your ears. It counts.

Mom wanted to call the doctor because I missed the bus and walked home from school by myself. Dad thought that wasn't the best idea. Mom said I don't think rules apply to me. That I don't actually think.

That hurt. After that, it got even worse.

Dad asked, "What do you want to do, ship him off to boarding school?"

Boarding school. As in, school I both go to and live at.

School away from family and friends and Zip.

I've disappointed them so much that they want me to go live someplace else.

I can't believe my ears. This whole time, I've tried my best to understand Mom and Dad and learn what makes them happy. It's been a challenge, for sure. Nothing I've done has helped. In fact, I think it may have made it worse.

I thought maybe my results hadn't been so great because they're mad at each other like Q said.

But I had it wrong. All wrong.

Just like when I showed them my room. I thought high quality time with their son would guarantee their happiness. All the cool things I do, what I'm interested in, all that stuff is in there. Parents love that kind of thing, right? They love their kid, so they're going to love looking at their favorite things. Or so I thought.

They didn't like anything they saw in my room. Not even a little bit.

It was unacceptable.

And now tonight.

I didn't mean to miss the bus. I didn't mean to upset

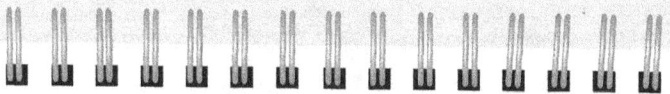

Sadie. None of this was supposed to happen. I guess the good thing, if there is a good thing, is at least now I know the truth.

It's not at all like Q said. I'm not grounded all the time because Mom and Dad are mad at each other.

I'm grounded all the time because they don't like *me*.

It isn't my room that's unacceptable.

It's me.

Chapter 31

This is a tough family to grow up in.

Set one fire, miss one bus, walk home one time? It's off to boarding school.

No do-overs. No takebacks. Just boarding school.

My insides are in knots. Those knots? Also knotted. I'm like a huge, tangled-up knot-ball on the inside.

I close my notebook. Sadie knocks and opens my bedroom door.

Her face is mucus-and-blotch-free. A fluffy pink overnight bag is slung over her shoulder. "Mom and Dad are taking me to Avery's sleepover. I'm not mad at you anymore."

One of the knots unwinds and I relax a tiny bit. "Thanks. And hey, I'm so sorry. I really didn't know about the, you know." I'm careful not to say *turtles* in case that word makes her cry again. "What are you guys going to do at Avery's?"

She brightens. "We're going to make jewelry and paint picture frames."

As horrible as that sounds? Still better than getting shipped off to boarding school. "Cool. Have a great time."

A giant, hairy lump forms in my throat.

Will Mom and Dad send me away tonight? What if this is the last time I see my big sister? Before I can stop myself, I hug her. Not a big bear hug, just a quick apology hug with a side of goodbye.

"Don't do anything else stupid while I'm gone." She hugs me back, then leaves.

I wait for Mom and Dad to give me yet another talking to before they drive Sadie to the party. But there's nothing. No stern warning to "stay in your room." No popping in to say, "We'll be right back, son."

Nothing. They've already forgotten about me.

Unreal.

I switch off the bedroom light and flop onto my bed. My face sinks deep into the cold pillow. If I could sink further, I would. There's not a squishy enough mattress in the world, though. That's how low I feel.

There's a level in FAH3 where you crawl through the desert. You're supposed to find the shady palm tree, so you don't, you know, get sun-sizzled.

But when you find the tree, guess what happens? That palm tree isn't an ordinary tree. It's the Buzzard Barracks. You're resting under the wings of a thousand hungry birds. Worst ambush ever.

That's what this feels like. I mean, I don't think Mom and Dad set a Buzzard Barrack-type of trap. Not on purpose, anyway. I just feel like I walked into one.

Stupid me thought I had actually managed to make Mom and Dad Somewhat Happy. We were having fun before dinner. Nobody argued. Everything was going great. I was going to tell them everything and they might have let me go to GamerCon. Things might have worked out.

But then I heard what they really think of me. It felt like I was the ant and they were the hungry buzzards.

Now what? If I tell them how I lied to Evan and Q now, that will make things even worse.

Or will it? Seriously, how can things get any worse? Mom and Dad are giving me the boot. I'm losing Evan and Q for sure because I'm going to boarding school and all.

It can't *get* worse.

So why can't I just go to GamerCon?

Just, you know, go?

Why not have one last, all-out gamer bonanza with my best friends at GamerCon before I lose them forever?

I flip over and sit bolt upright in the dark.

Would that be possible?

Mom and Dad got pretty upset when I walked home from school on my own. How mad would they get if I walked to the convention center by myself? Off the charts mad. Guaranteed Grounding times infinity. Probably.

But wait. They don't trust me anyway, right? They don't think I *think*. So who cares if they get mad again? If I went to GamerCon on my own, what's the worst thing that could happen? They'll send me to boarding school twice?

Ground me?

Maybe they won't even care. Because they're sending me away to be somebody else's problem. They don't want to be bothered by me and my danger-walking, not-thinking nonsense.

So I won't bother them.

I feel around on my night table for my bedside lamp. Click it on. Grab my notebook and pen. And write three more sentences in my field guide.

> Why does it matter if I make them happy?
> Why shouldn't I do whatever I want?
> I'm going to GamerCon with Evan and Q.

Chapter 32

I'm wide awake but it's dark outside. On a normal day, if I woke up at 4 a.m., I'd go right back to sleep. But today's no normal day.

In five hours, I'm leaving for GamerCon.

Here's my plan:

First things first: I need my phone. Yeah, yeah. I know I'm not supposed to have it. I'm not supposed to go to GamerCon either. But a kid's got to have a phone if he's sneaking across town. It's a safety issue. So I'll grab it out of the Forbidden Stuff Box (a.k.a. stuff Mom and Dad took from me) in the hall closet.

Next: Cash. I'll need to buy a ticket to GamerCon. A student ticket to GamerCon is $25, plus another $20 for snacks and souvenirs, maybe? I'll need at least $45. Last time I checked, I had like, $17.36 in my money jar. I hope Sadie's better at saving her allowance than I am because I'm raiding her pink narwhal bank. I'll write her a note that says:

> Dear Sadie,
>
> Please don't freak out. Mom and Dad are sending me away. And I'm going to GamerCon. I'll text you when I can.
>
> Thanks,
>
> Jeff
>
> PS I borrowed $50. I'll pay you back.
>
> PPS Sorry again about the you-know-whats yesterday.

Finally: Am I wearing pants? Shirt? Socks? Shoes? These things matter.

How will I get to GamerCon? Every Saturday morning, Mom and Dad go to the farmer's market. After they leave, I'll gather all my resources. I'll use my phone to look up the convention center address and get directions. I'll ride my bike to the convention center, buy a ticket, and have an amazing day with Evan and Q. When it's over, I'll ride home, take my punishment, and go to boarding school.

And that will be that.

Who says I don't think about anything?

Yellow sunlight peeks through my bedroom window. Pretty soon, I hear my door creak open. Silence. I assume Mom and Dad are taking notes and making plans for my room, you know, once they've booted me out. Then the door creaks closed again. A couple of minutes later, I hear car doors whump open and shut, the garage door whines up and down, and then quiet. They're gone.

And so my plan begins.

I raid the Forbidden Stuff box.

Ah. Hello, phone. I've missed you.

I loot Sadie's narwhal bank and leave my note on her pillow.

I ransack my clean laundry pile and get dressed.

Now for the logistics. I open the map app on my phone, type "city convention center" and hit 'directions.' Bingo. It's 16.4 miles away. I can bike 16.4 miles, and it probably wouldn't take me much more than, what, an hour to get there? That works, right?

Zip scratches at the back door, asking to go out. I unlatch the door and walk out back with him. The sky is grey and the air smells like rain. Perfect gaming weather. Zip brings me his tennis ball and we play. Toss. Run. Fetch. Drop.

Am I really doing this? Taking off solo? Going across town to meet up with friends? My gut feels tight and uncomfortable. I wonder if other criminal masterminds feel like they ate too much pizza. I mean, I'm not a *total* criminal mastermind. It's not like I'm stealing the Statue of Liberty or anything. I'm just breaking, like, a thousand house rules. First and foremost is the one about not leaving the house without a parent.

"He wants you to throw the ball again." Mrs. Fischer peeks over the back fence. She's smiling like she didn't wreck my life a couple of weekends ago. "The ball," she repeats.

I look down. The ball rests between my shoes. Zip wags his hind end.

"Thanks." I shake dirt off the ball and throw it at the back corner. Zip leaves clumps of dust on my ankles as he takes off.

"Is your sister okay?"

"She's fine. She *really* doesn't like turtles."

"Did you tell your mother to call me?"

Oops. "No, I'm sorry, I forgot."

"I see. That's alright." There's a long pause, then she asks, "Are you upset with me for calling the fire department?"

I shrugged. *How much cooler would my life be right now if she had stayed out of my business? Yes, I'm upset. I'm upset about a lot of things. But how do I say that to our neighbor?*

"A little."

"I thought you might be. I'm sorry for upsetting you. I worry when I see kids making dangerous choices."

Dangerous choices? That tight feeling in my chest returns, like my rib cage shrank. Words skip straight past my brain and tumble out of my mouth. "Why didn't you just talk to me? Why'd you have to call the fire department?"

"Who would you call if a house is on fire?"

"My house wasn't on fire, though." I grip the tennis ball to keep myself from throwing it at her.

"It was plenty close," Mrs. Fischer said. "Fire moves fast, son. It shows no mercy. You were lucky—"

A horn blast interrupts and I'm not sorry about it.

Mrs. Fischer jumps. "Oh! My driver is already here and look at me. Yapping in the backyard without my hair fixed or anything. I'm sorry you're upset but I'm glad you're safe. I hope someday you understand." She hustles toward her house.

She has a driver.

"Wait! Mrs. Fischer, wait!" The top of her head returns to the fence. "Did you say you have a ride?"

"Yes, my kids don't like me to drive myself places anymore."

"Where are you going?" I may not be president of the Mrs. Fischer fan club, but if it means getting to GamerCon? I can figure out how to get along with her.

"If you must know, a nice young man from church drives me to the grocery store and back every Saturday. And I'm being rude and keeping him waiting.'

"Could I ride with you? Please?" I use the politest voice I can manage.

"You want to go to the grocery store? Whatever for?"

"Well, not exactly to the grocery store. Someplace close by."

"Is it all right with your parents? If your parents approve, it's fine with me."

How can I avoid her question without lying? "My parents have already left for the farmer's market, but. . . there's someplace I'm supposed to be. . . ." Maybe she'll fill in the blanks on her own.

"Mmm. I see. Missed your ride, did you?"

"I missed it all right."

Kind of.

I wait another agonizing silent second.

Lord, please help, I don't want to lie again.

The horn honks again. She waves off the noise like she's swatting a fly. "I'm coming, I'm coming. Well, I'm sure Mr. Freeman won't mind one more passenger. Are you ready to go?"

"Yes ma'am."

Yes!

"Come on, then."

"Thank you, Mrs. Fischer!"

I just got a ride, but I feel like I could fly to GamerCon. I call Zip and we blaze inside.

Cash? Front left jeans pocket. Phone? Back right. Done. Check.

Zip leans against my shins like a cat. "Be a good boy, Zip."

A good boy. Ha. Would a good boy sneak out of his house? Lie to his friends? To Mrs. Fischer (sort of)? Take fifty bucks from his sister without permission? The knotball reappears in the pit of my belly, bigger and knottier than before.

I scoot Zip out of the way, grab the doorknob, and my gut lurches. What am I doing? Destroying any chance of being allowed to do anything until I'm what, thirty-five? Am I really doing this?

Hold up. What does it matter, anyway? They're about to dump me off at boarding school like an abandoned puppy. At least I'll get to have one perfect day with friends before I go. There's nothing wrong with that, is there?

I leave through the garage and put the door down behind me. Same as I would if I was going to hang out at the park with Evan and Q. Only this time I'm not going to the park. And there's that swooshy stomach/squeezy chest combo again.

Shake it off, Jeff. You've got friends to see and games to play.

A metallic gold minivan sits in Mrs. Fischer's driveway. Mrs. Fischer waves at me from her roost in the front passenger seat.

The main passenger door slides open and I jump in. A young, curly-headed guy smiles at me from behind the steering wheel. Mr. Freeman, I presume.

"Welcome aboard," says smiling guy. "You must be Jeff. I'm Lucas. Where you headed?"

"Thanks for the ride. I need to go to the Convention Center, please."

Please, Lucas, don't say it's too far. I cross my fingers.

"Cool. GamerCon?" He tugs the gearstick and the van rolls out of the driveway.

I nod and he continues. "Wish I could have gone this year, but it wasn't in the cards. Oh, well. There's always next year." He turns to Mrs. Fischer. "I think I'll drop your friend off first. Is that okay with you?"

"Yes, good, okay," she pokes at her phone. "That will give me time to finish my shopping list."

I let out a long breath and sink into the pleathery seat.

I'm doing it.

I can't believe it.

Is it possible to be both ridiculously happy and super nervous at the same time? What's the word for that feeling? I think it's hervous. Or nerpy. Whatever. All I know is that I want to dance and throw up at the same time.

GamerCon, here I come.

I pull my phone out of my pocket to text Q and Evan.

> Hey. I'm on the way. Meet you at the ticket office?

I wait for the three dots that show a response is coming.

Nothing.

It's okay. It's not like I expect them to be glued to their phones. You know, looking forward to my text. They'll respond when they see it. I watch the city landscape pass by the window, like a brick and concrete slideshow.

I check my phone again.

Still nothing. They're probably in the car with Evan's crazy siblings and not paying attention to their phones.

I imagine the moment when we meet up at the ticket office. They won't, you know, have balloons or cheer for me or anything. But it will be awesome. It will go something like this:

Q: Jeff! I knew you'd make it! Look, we bought matching T-shirts! Here's yours!

Evan: It's great to see you! What do you want to do first?

We'll explore every booth at GamerCon, win the Fire Ant Heroes 3 tournament, eat a whole extra-large pepperoni-and-sausage pizza, and take a ton of pictures together.

Maybe all of that happens. Or maybe none of that happens. We just walk around. I don't actually care what we do. I just want my friends and me to be together.

Once I'm with Evan and Q, I won't have to think about boarding school, parents, or anything. I won't have to be careful what I say or do. I won't have to try not to accidentally get in trouble.

All I have to do? Have an epic, super-fun farewell visit with my friends.

And pretend everything's going to be okay.

Chapter 33

The minivan slows to a stop at the curb by the convention center ticket office.

I launch myself out of the van. "Thank you!" Mr. Freeman and Mrs. Fischer wave goodbye.

I did it. Oh my gosh, I actually did it.

Excitement pulses through my veins, but nerves tap dance in my stomach. Super nerpy.

I inhale the Cheeto-scented air of GamerCon and scan the crowd. Where are Evan and Q? All I see is Halloween. People of all shapes, sizes, and costumes stream into the Convention Center. I join the line of superheroes, aliens, monsters, and who-knows-whatsits at the ticket booth.

This is something. I've never been to a convention center before. I've *definitely* never been to a convention center across town without my parents' knowledge or permission before. If the Mars Rover had feelings, this might be what it felt when it landed on Mars. I'm in uncharted territory.

When I find Evan and Q everything will be back to

normal. As normal as it gets, anyway, when you're about to be booted off to who-knows-where.

"One please," I say to the person dressed as a Minecraft creeper behind the Plexiglas.

Guilt pings off the back of my throat when I pull out my wallet. I exchange Sadie's cash for a QR access code and download my ticket.

Thank you, Sadie. I'll pay you back.

This is no time for guilt. This is GamerCon. I snap a victory selfie and text it to Evan and Q.

Beneath the pic, I see the words *delivered 10:07 a.m.* Then, three dots! That means one of them is typing something. I stare at the phone and bounce a little. I'm pretty sure that helps texts reach my screen faster.

The dots disappear.

They reappear.

Now the dots are gone.

They stay gone.

Probably a bad cell signal. I mean, there's what, thousands of people trying to use the Wi-Fi right now, right?

I try again.

> Hey guys. Where are you? I will come find you, just tell me where.

I stand on a bench and scan the crowd. It's hard not to get distracted by so many interesting-looking costumes, but I stay focused.

A stroller-pushing mom pulls up in front of me. "Sweetheart, please put your bottom on the chair. I don't want you to fall and get hurt."

"I'm okay. Thanks though."

She leans forward. "I'm not asking." She's not. Her "I-Mean-Business" voice is exceptionally clear. "Please sit down before you hurt someone. Where are your parents? Are you lost?"

Where are my parents, she asks? They're at the farmer's market. Pretty sure they're buying beets and celebrating my acceptance to boarding school. Does that make me lost? Sadness slides into my gut, but I shove it out.

"I'm really okay, but thanks." I hop off the bench.

She lingers for a moment. You know, to make sure I don't stand on the bench again. I don't. So she pushes the stroller into the crowd.

I check my phone one more time. No text from Evan or Q. Where are they? Maybe they're running late? They said they'd meet me at the ticket office, didn't they?

The nerpy nerves in my stomach stop tapping and start stomping.

Why don't they text? Where could they be?

I scan the crowd from left to right. Then right to left. Closest to farthest. Farthest to closest. I repeat this process ten times. No luck.

Have they texted me back yet? Nope.

I count people wearing Fire Ant Heroes 3 costumes. There are 47. None of them are my friends.

It's 10:45. I search the crowd for the bazillionth time. No luck.

I rack my brain for clues. A while back, Evan, Q, and I had planned to compete in the Fire Ant Heroes tournaments. Maybe they did that without me—only because they didn't know for sure I'd be here. I'm sure there was like, a registration deadline or something. No biggie.

The stomping in my belly transforms into soaring. *Of course.* That has to be where they are. They're in a tournament and lost track of time. If they're using all the tips I taught them, they're probably winning. And wondering why I'm not there cheering for them.

I send Evan and Q a message:

> Waited at ticket window like we said. Til 10:47. Going to find FAH3 tournament. If you're not there already, meet me there.

I step into the stream of people, elbow-to-elbow with someone dressed like Pikachu. We flow through the convention center lobby toward the exhibit hall entrance. The digital sign above says WELCOME TO GAMERCON.

Music and laughter pulse all around. I show my QR code to a lady dressed in green, and she wraps a blue band around my wrist. She smiles and says something I can't hear. I smile back, though. Then step into the wall-to-wall sea of people.

A tall, hairy-costumed person accidentally whacks me in the face with their tote bag. Twice. The heavy, sweet scent of fried dough mixes with sweaty people smell. The aroma hangs in the air and I think it makes walking harder.

By the time I reach the GamerCon Info booth, I totally

get why traffic makes Dad so grumpy.

My stomach aches at the thought of my dad. Or maybe it's the sweaty people smell. Probably both. But neither is my mission. My mission is to find Evan and Q at the FAH3 tournament. I grab a map and inspect it. Where are the tournaments?

The exhibit hall is divided into four sections: Art and Artists, Console Lounge, Arcade Games, and Tabletop. I flip the map over and see a block of conference rooms highlighted with the words Tournament Row. Perfect.

My back pocket vibrates. Hope buzzes in my chest for the first time since this morning. I have a text! Finally!

Aw, man. It's from Nic.

Sadie called me. You're at GamerCon????

A thousand questions flood my head. Why did Sadie call Nic, of all people? Who else did Sadie call? Why didn't she call me? Maybe she did and I didn't hear it ring. If Sadie's home, does that mean my parents are home too? My heart drops into a dunk tank of dread.

Do I text her back? She'll just give me another lecture about who I can and can't be friends with. Thank you, no. Hard pass. I only have a few hours with Evan and Q before my one-way ticket to boarding school arrives. I don't want to waste it arguing with Nic.

The map says the escalator to Tournament Row is near the back of the Arts and Artists section. Why isn't anything in this place easy to get to?

I jostle through the crowds past colorful booths.

Framed prints and sculptures of my favorite gaming characters line the walkway. If I wasn't in such a hurry, I'd check them out. But Evan and Q are waiting for me. No time to waste.

Near the center of the section, there's a small stage for character meet and greets. Pay $20 to take a selfie with people dressed in costumes? I don't get it.

My phone buzzes again and I sneak a peek. Still Nic. *Back to the pocket, phone.*

I get closer to the stage, and I have to admit it. The setup is pretty sweet. It's decorated to look like a boss battle scene from Fire Ant Heroes 3. Plus, the characters in this meet and greet are Sergeant Sting, Queen Adlee, and Tromma Tize. No wonder the line is super long.

I hustle past, steal a glance at two kids cheesing it up with the characters onstage. They're wearing matching Sergeant Sting t-shirts and antennae headbands. Their phones are out, snapping selfie after selfie.

It's Evan and Q.

Finally! I steamroll my way to the side of the stage. The hope bubble is back and floatier than ever. The three of us can spend the rest of the afternoon hanging out like old times.

"Hey! There you are! I've been looking all over for you guys!" I hold my hand up for a celebratory high five.

Evan and Q freeze like they got caught robbing a bank. Evan's mouth drops open in a giant "O." They're hilarious.

"Jeff?" Q's antennae bobble.

"What are you doing here?" Evan asks.

"I told you I was coming, didn't I? Didn't you get my texts?" I lower my hand. *Guess we'll come back to that high five.*

"I didn't think you were serious," Evan says.

"Why wouldn't I be serious? I told you yesterday I was coming. We've been talking about it for months."

Why aren't they glad to see me? Aren't we best friends?

Evan scoffs. "Yeah. Like you didn't lie yesterday at lunch. Your parents already told my parents you weren't coming, like a week ago."

"Yeah? I'm here, aren't I? I said I'd be here and I'm here. Did my parents *also* tell your parents they're sending me to boarding school?" I pause so they can respond appropriately. Tears would be nice. General sadness? Also acceptable. But they just stand there in their matching t-shirts.

Q breaks the awkward silence. "When are you leaving?"

Somewhere inside my chest, the hope bubble turns to glass and shatters.

"I tell you I'm being shipped off to boarding school and all you want to know is *when*? I thought you were my best friends."

"You thought wrong," Evan says. "You call us your best friends, but you treat us like your sidekicks."

"I do not!" I shout.

"You know what? You're right." Evan says. "You don't

treat us like sidekicks. It's worse. You're like a bulldozer. You run right over everybody else and do whatever you want. You don't care about the people around you. You only think of yourself."

"This is not factually accurate. Like, at all. Q, come on, back me up. This isn't true."

"He's kind of right. I mean, we've had fun sometimes. But most of the time, it's really hard to be your friend." Q adjusts his glasses and stands taller.

My face stings like I've been slapped. My skin burns and crawls from the inside out. I want to yell at him, at both of them. But there's no air in my throat and I can't make words with my mouth.

All I can do is stand by myself next to the stage and watch their antennae wobble as they walk away.

Chapter 34

"Excuse me, will you take our picture please?" A purple-maned unicorn asks, posing with its pink-maned unicorn buddy.

I'm not sure how long I've been standing here next to the stage, but the unicorn's polite question yanks me back to reality.

I nod, snap a few photos, and pass the phone back without a word. There's not much for me to say to unicorns or to anyone else.

My parents are shipping me off to who-knows-where.

My best friends think I'm the worst and dumped me in front of the entire GamerCon world.

I have no idea how I'm getting home.

After what I've done today, will I even be allowed home?

These are not topics for discussion with happy unicorns. Zombies, maybe. But not unicorns.

I wander the convention center, trying to make sense of what happened.

Evan called me a bulldozer. What does that even mean? He said I don't care about anyone but myself. How can he think that I don't care about my friends? All I wanted was to have fun with my best friends.

Everything I've done for weeks has been so I could hang out with them. That's all I wanted. Sneaking out, stealing from Sadie, lying to Mrs. Fischer. Basically breaking the biggest rules of them all. I did all of it so I could have one epic day with my best friends.

And it was all for nothing.

I wander until I end up in tournament row. I'm behind a kid in a crocodile costume, in a slow-moving line for a game called "Pitfall." I've never heard of this game. If a kid in a crocodile suit wants to play it, that's good enough for me.

I plop into a seat in the last row and stew some more.

It's not like Evan and Q are perfect. Nic and Vince sure don't think so. Even Mrs. P noticed something was weird. They *were* kind of rude during Science Club, weren't they? Evan pegged me in the head with a pink giant eraser. Not cool.

They totally laughed at me when I concussed myself on a lasagna noodle in the cafeteria. And they're the ones who ditched me at lunch. Twice. They even joined a soccer team without me.

Not to mention, you know, what they did today.

I hitched a ride with Mrs. Fischer and snuck out of my house to be here. They said we'd meet at the ticket office.

So I go to the ticket office. They're not there. But *I'm* hard to be friends with?

None of those things are what best friends do. Best friends include each other, they don't leave each other behind. How did I not see it before? Mrs. P was right. What people do is way more important than what they say. And what Evan and Q did wasn't nice.

I scrub the stupid tears out of my eyes.

Get it together, Jeff. You're at GamerCon.

In my head, I elbow jab thoughts of Evan and Q out of my skull. I zero in on the screen and focus on Pitfall. It's no Fire Ant Heroes 3, but it looks like it might be fun. If you like games from back in the 1990s, I guess.

You guide Pitfall Harry through the jungle to collect treasure before time runs out. If you're not careful, Harry falls into a tunnel with a scorpion-looking creature. The puddles in this game have crocodiles in them. So, not super-realistic. But if you fall, you just find your way out with ladders or rope swings. The name of the game for Pitfall Harry is to keep moving forward.

The lights blare on and everyone files out of the room. Well, everyone except me. I don't have any place to go. I'm Pitfall Harry. Stuck in the pit. No ladder or rope swing in sight.

But I have to keep going. I watch a GamerCon host pick up trash and straighten chairs in the row ahead of me. Maybe I could do that. Skip the boarding school thing and go work for GamerCon. Travel around, play games.

Start over.

"Hey." The host smiles as he makes his way down my row. "Sorry, but we gotta get the room ready for the next round."

"Oh, sure." I rub my eyes as they adjust to the brightness. "No problem."

He squints. "Are you okay, man?"

Not really, no, GamerCon Guy. "Uh, yeah. I was just, you know, thinking. How do you get a job here?"

"You looking for free games? Because I gotta tell you, they don't give the games away like they used to."

"No, no. I mean, free games would be sweet and all, but no. I just. . . ." Do I tell a total stranger I *messed up bad and I can't go home?* I stare at the floor, looking for the right words.

"You have to be sixteen to work the tournaments or the floor, and you have to be twenty-one to work the food service area."

Sixteen? That's forever from now. My disappointment must be streaming from my face because the guy says "I think sometimes they need volunteers for tabletop games. That's how I started. You might talk with them."

"Cool, thanks." I check my map. "I'll give it a shot."

All I know is I need a fresh start.

My stomach growls and my feet throb as I make my way out of tournament row. There's a snack bar next to a flashing checkerboard sign that says Tabletop Games. I count my—Sadie's—cash. I have enough for a hotdog and lemonade. But I'm not sure about how I'll eat tomorrow. Or the next day. Maybe GamerCon feeds their volunteers.

I buy my last meal and sit on the floor beneath the counter.

Whether it's the convention center hot dog or my mixed-up life, I don't know, but my belly churns.

My phone vibrates again. I wipe my hands on my jeans and check my texts. Two new messages from Nic are waiting for me.

> Sadie called and said you went to GC and your parents are sending you away? Call me back.

Fifteen minutes later, she wrote:

> JEFF WHERE ARE YOU CALL ME BACK

Why did Sadie have to open her big mouth and blab to Nicole, of all people? Ugh. None of this was supposed to happen. How did I manage to get everything so wrong?

I take a deep breath and text Nic back.

> Yes, I'm at GamerCon. Too loud in here to call. Tell Sadie not to worry.

I hit send and put the phone back in my pocket. I slurp watered-down lemonade and watch peoples' shins parade past the counter. Next thing I know, a familiar pair of purple leggings stops in front of me.

"Tell her yourself."

Chapter 35

Last time I saw these purple leggings I was flat on my back in the cafeteria.

That day, my best friends laughed at me until they cried. Today?

Things are different.

Today I don't have best friends at all.

I nudge her black Converse with my toe. "Hey."

She grabs my ankle and pulls me into the light. "What is wrong with you? Your family is freaking out."

I massage the splotchy red bracelet her grip left on my ankle. "What else is new?"

Nic gives me her cut-it-out glare and I know she's not playing. She's really upset.

I sigh. "Fine. What did Sadie tell you?"

"She said you left her a note that your parents are sending you someplace, and you were going to GamerCon. What does that even mean? Where're Quenton and Evan?"

Tears blur my vision. I can't even hear their names without feeling like garbage. No way can I tell Nic what happened. I mop my eyes before she can see them and push myself to my feet. "I don't know. Somewhere around here, I guess. Who are you here with?"

"Mom and Morgan, my little sister." She waves to a smiling lady and a preschool-aged girl playing checkers at a table. "Vince is going to meet us later. So, you haven't seen Q and Evan? Who are you here with? Can you hang out for a while? When Vince gets here, maybe we can find that new Fire Ant spinoff game, Wasp Wizard."

I ignore her first question. But hanging out with Nicole? I guess it's better than sulking under a table by myself.

"Cool. Sure." I follow her through the crowd. We weave past tables full of hard-core Dungeons and Dragons gamers, enthusiastic Risk players, and Catan conquistadors. Nic snatches a deck of cards from a giant stack of games. We sit at our own table near her family.

"Uno?" That's probably my least favorite game of all time.

A groan starts in my throat, but then I hear Evan's voice in my head. "You're a bulldozer. Friendless bulldozer Jeff," it says. A picture pops into my mind of him and Q playing soccer. It makes my insides feel swampy. I don't want that picture anymore. "Do you want to shuffle, or do you want me to?"

"I'll shuffle." She swooshes the cards between her fingers and deals the hand. "So?"

"So what?"

"Are you going to tell me what happened? Where are you going? How come your parents are sending you away?" She plays a +4 card.

"There's not much to tell. Mom's mad. Dad suggested boarding school. So that's that." I shrug, like *yeah, it stinks but I'm handling it like a champ.*

"That's *so not* that." She squints. "Your mom and dad are sending you to boarding school. You've been grounded for forever, but suddenly it's okay for you to go to GamerCon with Evan and Quenton? And now, you're here—but you don't know where they are?"

I lay down a wild card. "Green." She draws.

We sit in silence for a moment. Nic looks at the cards in her hand, then at me. "Well?"

What do I say about today? Do I make something up, or tell her the truth? I lied before and nothing good happened. But will anything good happen if I tell the truth? Will she laugh at me? Will she say 'I told you so?' I stare at the discard pile and wrestle with my thoughts.

She taps the table. "It's your turn."

I don't want to be that lying guy anymore. Besides, what's the worst that can happen? I'll probably never see Nic again anyway. Might as well tell her how it really is. I lay down a green two. "You missed the part about me accidentally traumatizing Sadie because I didn't know she was afraid of turtles. And that my parents think I'm hopeless. Oh—and Evan and Q told me I'm a terrible friend." My voice crackles. "That's why I don't know where they are.

They don't want me around." I wait for her to laugh, but she doesn't.

Instead, she rests her hands on the table. "I'm sorry. That stinks."

We're quiet for a second. Then Nic looks me in the eyes, super-intense, like she's about to drop some serious life wisdom. "Jeff?"

"Yeah?"

"Uno."

We crack up, and everything feels a little lighter. She deals again. I lose again. It's such a good time that I don't even care that I don't win. I'm actually having a blast playing cards with Nicole Norris.

After a while, Nic's mom asks us if we'd mind getting the four of us some drinks. The snack bar line is probably 50 people long when we join it.

Nic teaches me the fine art of people watching while we wait. It's way more entertaining than observing and not at all like stalking. Observing is science. Stalking is creepy. People watching? It's like watching YouTube without sound or captions.

"Ooooh. Jackpot. Look. Guy dressed like a dragon at two o'clock." Nic bounces on her toes. I follow her gaze and she's right. A huge, fuzzy, red dragon appears to be deep in conversation with a purple platypus. "What's he saying? Go."

"Um, well, clearly they know each other, and he's got something important to say. He's like, 'You shall play the

Final Story 14 tournament with me, and you will like it, platypus.'" I even use a deep, growly, dragon-y voice for extra drama.

Nic mimics the platypus's hand gestures. "I shall not indeed, good dragon. I have a secret mission to infiltrate the Sewer Wars and capture the Plunger of Ultimate Doom. Doooom, I say."

I'm about to dial up the dragon conflict when I see them. Out of the corner of my eye, I catch a blurry glimpse of my parents and Sadie. They pinball their way through the crowd, pinging from one group of people to the next.

My insides feel like a whole hive of wasps have moved in. My head buzzes.

"I gotta go." I only make it a half step in the other direction before Nic strong-arms me back into place.

"Nope. The only place you gotta go is to talk to them."

The buzzing swarm in my head intensifies. "*Talk* to them? There's no talking to them. There's *They Send Me to Boarding School*." I wrench myself out of Nic's grasp.

She shoves me—gently—out of line, toward the source of my pain. "Go, dork." If she's worried that she'll never see me again, she doesn't show it. "It's okay. It will be okay."

I'm not so sure. How can she stay this calm? My insides have liquified. I take a last look at Nic, then me and my jelly legs walk toward my family.

For probably the millionth time today, I have no clue what to say. I'm all mixed up inside. Even though I know they're ready to boot me to wherever, part of me is relieved to see them. Another part of me—a bitter, chunky, piece that seems to be caught in my throat right now—knows that if they could teleport me to space and never see me again, they would.

Chapter 36

Mom sees me first. "Jeffrey? Jeffrey!" The whole family rushes at me like ants swarming a veggie chip. Then arms, so many arms, wrap around me and squeeze. This is not the yell-fest I expected.

"We were worried sick," Dad says. His voice is watery. Is he crying?

"I'm so glad you're okay." Mom sniffles and grips my shoulders, steps back, and—oh—here's the glare I was expecting. "I don't know what you were thinking, pulling a stunt like this."

"If you thought you were grounded before...," Dad piles on. I knew that was coming.

Sadie slugs me in the arm. "Where's my fifty dollars?"

Nic's laugh bounces over the crowd. *Of course, she's watching.*

"*Say-dee*, no hitting. Let's go. We'll talk at home." Mom wraps an arm around my shoulder and takes Sadie by the hand. Dad pulls the three of us close. Then he shepherds us out of the bustling convention center.

The walk out to the car feels like a carnival ride. Not the whirly, twirly, pukey kind. The kind that creeeeps to the top of a tower. Then it stops. And then that awful, exciting-but-terrifying moment when you notice how waaaay far off the ground you are. When you're excited and terrified and then the floor drops and you drop with it.

That's where I am. Stuck in that one, waiting-for-the-floor-to-drop moment.

When we climb into the car it's silent. Mom sniffles every few seconds. But otherwise, nothing.

It seems like there should be yelling. But no one speaks the entire drive home. Not even Sadie.

Fat raindrops begin to fall as Dad pulls the car into the garage and turns off the engine. Mom and Sadie exit the car without a word, but Dad turns to face me. "Leave your phone on the kitchen table and go wait in your room. Mom and I will be there in a minute." He's not mean about it, but he's definitely all business.

I do what Dad says.

Any minute now, Mom and Dad are going to walk into my room. *My room.* My perfect place. The one thing about me that I thought would impress Mom and Dad. Ha. Boy was I wrong. I guess it won't be mine for much longer, will it?

They'll storm in here and tell me if I can't do things right, that I don't belong. And then they'll hand me my ticket to Canada. Or maybe Detroit. I don't actually know where boarding schools are. I just know I'm going. The knot-boulder growing in my belly confirms it.

So I guess it's time to say my goodbyes. So long, writing desk. Goodbye, science fair medals. Farewell, laboratory. Adios, remnants of my mushroom farm. I want to remember every possible detail of your gloriousness. You know, before Mom and Dad turn you into a boring old guest room or something.

I ought to start packing. I drag my old gym bag out from beneath my bed. It's from third grade, so it's kind of small, but that's fine. I don't have a lot of clothes to pack anyway. I grab a handful of socks and stuff them in the bag. Packing feels like I'm punching myself in the gut, but I do it anyway. I manage to get two piles of socks and underpants in the bag and then Mom and Dad walk in.

My heart jackhammers against my rib cage. They file past me and sit on my bed. Dad's arms are crossed like a Supreme Court Justice. Mom's face is red and blotchy beneath the rim of her pink baseball cap. It's time for my sentencing. I grip the gym bag hard, stare at my big toe and wait for the floor to drop.

"Look at me, Jeff." I breathe deep. Force myself to look Dad in the eyes. There's a slow burn in them, but the fire isn't anger. This expression? It's not on my Visual Guide.

"You were very lucky today."

Is he serious? I sure don't feel lucky. At all.

As I open my mouth to express how one-hundred-percent-the-opposite-of-lucky I am, Dad continues.

"You betrayed our trust, leaving the house like that."

He speaks precisely. Like he's building a tower brick by brick.

"Dad, I'm—"

"Let me finish. Mrs. Fischer told us she gave you a ride to the convention center. If she hadn't done that, what was your backup plan? I assume you had a backup plan."

Of course, Mrs. Fischer talked to my parents. I nod. "I was going to ride my bike."

"Your bike? You were going to bike the—what, fifteen miles—by yourself, across the highway?" He squeezes his eyes tight and presses his hand against his mouth. "Do you understand how incredibly dangerous that is? Do you understand that being at the convention by yourself was *not safe*? You've made questionable decisions before, but this is. . . . What in the world were you thinking? *Were* you thinking? *At all*?"

Each question is louder and sharper than the one before it. Each word pokes at my bones. Who broke whose trust, exactly? Last time I checked, parents aren't supposed to plot against their kids. They're not supposed to ship their kids off to who knows where. They're supposed to love me. Not send me away.

Rage clamps onto my chest and squeezes. Hard. So hard that I throw my half-full gym bag at my bedroom door. The impact sends socks and underwear sailing across my room.

"You have no idea what I've been thinking! Even if you did—what do you care? You're just getting rid of me anyway! I'm some boarding school's problem now, not yours, right? So why does it matter to you?"

Dad's face flushes redder than a stoplight. He clenches his mouth until his lips disappear.

Tears spill from the corners of his eyes. "It matters because you matter. When your mom and I came home and you weren't here, and then Sadie found your note?" He coughs. "You didn't answer our calls or texts. We had no idea if you were okay. I was living my worst nightmare." Mom rubs Dad's shoulder and nods.

I stare at the scattered wads of underthings on my floor. I didn't know they called or texted. I imagine my parents coming home from the market. Finding my room empty. I pick up a stray sock and twist it in my hands.

Dad dries his face on his shirtsleeve. "I'm thankful that you're alright. But I'm furious with you for putting yourself in harm's way. I expect better decisions from you because I love you and I need you to be safe."

The last time I saw Dad cry was when Grandma Pennant passed away. Watching him now makes my insides heavy. Knowing I hurt him is like a giant, wet blanket over my brain. But knowing their plan to abandon me weighs me down even more.

Mom pulls something out of her back pocket. My stomach lurches. It's my notebook.

They have my notebook.

She leans against Dad's shoulder. "Mrs. Peddy emailed us last night. She suggested we talk with you about your book. We'd planned to ask you about it this morning." She swipes tears from her eyes with the back of her hand.

A couple of days ago I would have been furious about Mrs. P betraying me like this. Right this second, though, it only stings at tiny-annoying-honeybee level. Not murder-hornet-agonizing-pain. Mostly because Mom and Dad already have that covered.

Mom collects herself. "We wouldn't have read it without your permission, but we were desperate. We thought if we read what you wrote, it might give us some clues about where you'd gone."

Dad takes the notebook from Mom and flips through the pages. "You only heard part of our conversation, but you still believed we would send you away. Why?"

"You said you would. That's what I believed. And you act like you want to. You're mad at me all the time."

"*All* the time? We're not mad at you all the time. Even if we were—even if we *were* talking about boarding school—sneaking out like that? That is not okay. I don't care how upset you are, running away is never the answer. That could have been a permanent solution to a temporary problem. We were very lucky to have found you." Dad looks at the ceiling for a second and clears his throat. "And for the record, we're not sending you to boarding school."

It takes a moment for his words to sink in. When they do, though, I feel like I just leveled up on FAH3. No, wait. It's a hundred times better than that. I wipe a fresh stream of tears from my cheeks and choke out two words. "You're not?"

A half-smile wobbles across Dad's face. "No. Not even close."

"But you said—"

"You missed the end of the conversation, my man. That was the best part. Mom and I agreed that yes, sometimes you and your sister can both be a challenge. But we love you. And we like you. A lot. Even if we think your room's a mess."

Mom takes my hand in hers. "You're not going to boarding school. You *are* still grounded for running off like that. And you'll do extra chores to pay back the money you took from Sadie. But you're stuck with us, buddy."

My tears go from stream to tsunami in a split second. Mad and hurt wash out of my system all at once. Crying is like a reset button.

I get a fresh start.

Mom scooches down to the floor next to me and dries my tears with a stray sock. "I read what you wrote about your dad and I fighting. About how you're worried we're getting a divorce. We're not."

Dad sits on the other side of me. "We might not be fun anymore, but we're not getting a divorce." Mom pokes him in the ribs. "Ouch! We're fine. Everything's fine. We're all fine."

Mom kisses my forehead. "I wish you would have talked with us about how you felt."

Mrs. P's words float across my memory. *Occam's*

Razor. The simplest answer to a problem is likely the best. She was right. What would have happened if I'd talked with Mom and Dad? About everything?

Mom smiles sadly from behind blotchy cheeks. Dad rubs his red-rimmed eyes. I've scared them. Not a silly jump-scare, either. It's a can't-eat-or-sleep type of afraid. Because they love me.

A hot chunk of awful drops into my belly. "I'm so, so sorry. I never should have run away."

"Promise me. The next time you're upset about something, we'll talk it out." Dad says. "No more running away. We're a team."

I thought Evan and Q were my friends. My team. When one person on the team is having a hard time, doesn't it affect the rest of the team? They didn't act like it. Does a team ditch each other for lunch? Do they laugh when a friend falls?

But Mom and Dad are different. They're on my side, even when I mess up. We're a real, unstoppable team. The kind that talks things out. The kind that does what they say they'll do.

I nod. "I promise."

"I promise, too." Mom sniffles. "You've noticed, I think, these past few months at work have been hard for me. Pretty brutal, actually. I've taken it out on everyone and I shouldn't have, I'm sorry."

"It's okay, Mom." I squeeze her hand. Then I remember my Jar-Jar accent and I flinch. "I asked you why you didn't quit your job. Oh, man. I made it worse."

Dad fist bumps me and says "You-sa gets it, brudda."

"Wait. That's why you left the table? Because I was right?"

She shakes her head. "I left because my struggle didn't need an audience."

"I'm not an audience." I hug Mom with everything my arms can give. "I'm your son. I'll always struggle with you."

She laughs and squeezes me tight. "Right back at'cha, kiddo. And you know what?" She releases the hug and holds my hands. "I don't think you made it worse. Even though it was hard to hear, your question helped. I was so upset, your dad and I talked almost all night. And I decided—well, *we* decided something. We've been waiting for the right time to tell you and Sadie."

"Tell us what?"

Mom's face shines. "I'm quitting my job. I'm going back to college and finishing my degree. I'm going to be a teacher."

Dad leans behind me and squeezes Mom's shoulder. Right now, according to my Visual Scale of Parental Happiness, they are off the charts happy. Dad beams. Mom's face is one hundred percent grin, and I can't help but grin along with her. "That's awesome, Mom!"

"There are going to be big changes around here, especially when Mom's classes start. You and your sister will need to step up. But we know you can do it." Dad wraps his arms around Mom and me and pulls us tight.

We huddle in our happiness cocoon for a long time before Mom and Dad leave me to put away my now-very-unpacked underpants. Even though they left the room, I still feel their warmth around my shoulders.

I'm not sure what types of 'big changes' Dad is talking about, but right now I don't even care. If big changes are what it takes to see Mom and Dad smile like this?

I'll work it out.

HOW TO RAISE HAPPY PARENTS
by JEFF PENNANT

CHAPTER SIX

I started this field guide with a theory. I thought if I could figure out what made my parents happy, I'd spend less time grounded and more time living my best life.

The best news is that my parents are happier than ever. You know how they used to always waffle between Steer Clear, Proceed With Extreme Caution, and Guaranteed Grounding? They don't do that so much anymore. Now, they spend most of their time bouncing around between the Somewhat Happy and Full Happy stages, with only occasional dips into Proceed With Extreme Caution.

In scientific terms, I'd call this a success.

But I'm still grounded.

I'm not mad about it, though. Well, maybe I am a little irritated. Nobody likes being grounded. That's factually accurate. Still, I know I messed up big time. I didn't exactly

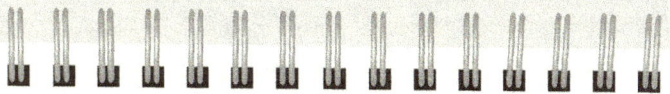

expect balloons and cake after what I did.

It's been two weeks since the GamerCon disaster. And I have to say they've been two pretty decent weeks. I might not be allowed to have my phone or my games or have people over yet, but believe it or not, I've been kind of having fun. Because that's what I do.

School's been okay without Evan and Q. I've been sitting with my friends Nic and Vince at lunch. In a couple of weeks, when I'm ungrounded, they're coming over to play Uno. I told them all about this book, and they can't wait to buy a copy. They're pretty cool that way. I even told them about an idea I had, and they helped me make a chart for it.

It's a chart of things I do that make Mom and Dad happy.

CHART 1: THINGS THAT MAKE MOM AND DAD HAPPY
by JEFF PENNANT

The thing I did	Mom	Dad	Notes
Extra chores to pay Sadie's money back AND buy her the glitter markers she wanted.	😊	😊	I thought I'd get Sadie something to make up for the whole t-u-r-t-l-e thing. Sadie liked it. So did Mom and Dad.
I ate eggplant. On purpose.	😊	😊	If the farmers market has fresh eggplant, Mom and Dad talk about it all weekend. I refused to try it for so long they stopped offering. Last time Dad grilled it, I tried a slice. It wasn't Jim Junior's, but it wasn't, like, I-have-to-throw-up-right-now either. Mom and Dad were so happy, they gave me extra dessert.

On Sunday before church, I made them coffee the way they like it. Kind of.	Mom likes almond milk lattes with extra whipped cream.	Dad likes black coffee, room temperature.	Sadie operated the coffeepot. I was in charge of the milk, sugar, and whipped cream. I put too much sugar in Mom's but she said it was a nice treat. Dad's was super easy, and he drank three cups.
I have a recorder concert next week and I practiced in the garage instead of the living room.	☺	☺	Mom gave me a cookie before dinner.
I asked if we could take a family walk to the park after dinner.	☺	☺	They liked it so much now we do it every Tuesday. (We avoid the creek because of the you-know-whats.)

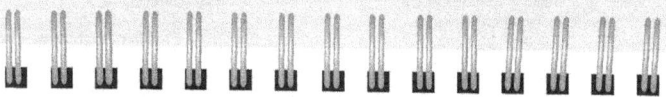

Every day, I do something to see if I can make them smile. If it works? I write it on my chart. I don't do big, over-the-top things like order them matching diamond-studded bracelets off the internet. I can't afford that. Also, I'm not allowed on the computer without a parent. It's not about buying them stuff, anyway. It's about finding little ways to do nice things for my team.

Like yesterday, for example. I set my alarm fifteen minutes early and got ready for school extra fast. Then I wrote two *haikus*—one for Mom, one for Dad. I snuck Dad's into his lunch bag and taped Mom's to the coffeepot.

Sadie's even getting into it. She and I are making a study schedule for Mom. Mom's classes don't start until after the summer, but we're helping her get ready anyway. (I think Sadie just likes using the new glitter markers I bought her).

I'm not doing things to get ungrounded faster or earn more allowance. I'm not even trying to make them happy so they'll give me screen time sooner. (Although all of that would be super cool) I'm doing it because of that night I made dinner with them.

After our GamerCon talk, I thought about that night a

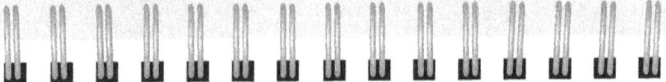

lot. That night was the happiest I'd seen Mom and Dad in a long time. Dad was cracking his awful jokes, and Mom was humming, and we all had a great time (pre-turtle discovery, anyway).

I know stuff like making dinner with your family isn't theme-park or GamerCon-type awesome. It isn't flashy. Nobody gets medals at the end. But I think it's cool. That night, at least for a little while, me, Mom, and Dad worked together and had fun. We laughed a lot. Who doesn't like doing that?

It's not about who has the most achievements or levels up the fastest. When you're part of a team, what affects one person affects the team. Little things count as much as the big ones. Maybe even more.

Talking out feelings when something's bothering you. Forgiving when someone makes mistakes. Finding ways to help.

That's how you raise happy parents.

Chapter 38

Exactly two months after GamerCon, the best gaming tournament ever is happening. Now. In my backyard. After a three-round Uno battle, we've moved on to a little game Nic made up called Slingbean. Sadie is the referee.

"On your mark!" Sadie yells from the back fence.

Nic, Vince, and I line up—with our slingshots—at the edge of the patio.

"Nic's toe is over the edge!" Vince shouts.

"No it's not! Let's go!" Nic shouts back. She's right. Her foot is nowhere near the edge. Still, she scooches ever so slightly backward just to be safe.

"Slingshots ready!" Sadie hollers.

I load a blue beanbag into my slingshot. Stretch the band as far and as tight as I can pull. Nic and Vince do the same.

"Winner picks the next game, right?" I look over at my friends.

Vince nods. "Loser wears the turkey hat."

Nic grins. "I like the turkey hat."

"Fire!" Sadie dashes to the corner of the yard as the three of us shout and let go of our bands. Beanbags sail through the air. Zip races in circles.

Vince's green bag smacks the back fence. "Boom!" He high fives me. "Did it! It's about time!"

Nic's yellow bag rockets way up into the old maple tree by the shed. Twigs and leaves fall to the ground. "Woah! I totally meant to do that."

My blue bag? Spluttered and plopped about halfway across the yard. Possibly the most spectacular fail in Slingbean history.

"What do you want to play next?" As if I need to ask Vince.

"Are you guys up for some FAH?" Vince says it 'fah,' instead of F-A-H. And he says it like a burp so it's extra awesome.

"Oh, I guess." Nic pretends she doesn't like FAH. But we know better. She's probably the biggest gamer of all of us. She's elite level on like, every game we play.

Sadie jogs over and drops the foam turkey hat on my noggin. "Gobble, gobble!"

I wear the hat inside and we spend the rest of the afternoon FAH-ing, eating pizza, and generally being awesome. Because that's what we do.

Nic's parents and Vince's parents show up to pick them up. I ask Mom and Dad if we can have a few minutes to take some photos together while the parents all talk. Mom and Dad say yes and high five me.

We take one photo with silly faces. Another one super serious, like, no smiling allowed. Turkey hat and all. Which is kind of hilarious. Then a for-real one, with everyone smiling.

Especially me.

Acknowledgments

My lands, a lot of people helped shape this book. First and foremost, I'm thankful to God for His gift of words and the people who love them.

Huge thanks to my earliest early readers, who saw me through Jeff's Angsty/Ranty stage: Avery White, Lori Z Scott, Cristy Sydow, Chryssa Keenon, Bethany Jett, Johnnie Alexander, Lyn Freeman, and Heather Burress. High fives to my SCBWI-NT Roots Coffeehouse crew who helped me find Jeff's voice: Rebecca Balcárcel, Jackie Kruzie, Alan Elliott, and Ted Perotti. The biggest, hugest hugs to the best critique partners a Covid-trapped aspiring writer could ever ask for: Marie Sontag, Glenda Simmons, Andrea Rand, Debby Spitzer, Sabra Girard, and Carla Conorino. You're proof that iron sharpens iron. A special extra bonus thank you to miss Morgan Girard.

Kiri Jorgensen, I'm still over the moon that you saw something in Jeff and believed this little story had a chance. Thank you. Wyn Batton, thank you for bringing Jeff's story to life with your incredible art.

My husband David and our son Aidan had breakfast for dinner oh-so-many nights because of this book. I publicly thank them and love them for this and a gazillion other reasons. You've blessed me beyond measure.

Everyone should have people in their lives like my siblings/siblings-in-law: Michael, Amanda, Heather, Josh, Brooke, John, Lynn, Kathy, and David - your support and encouragement have been monumental. Thank you. Ginormous thank you hugs to all my fam –cousins, aunts, uncles, nieces, nephews, and of course, to my parents. Smiling toward Heaven for Grandma and for Grammy, both of whom I miss with all my heart, and both of whom would have loved this journey. Best. Family. Ever.

Finally, if you're reading this, please know that I am sincerely grateful for you. I wrote this book to make you smile.

xoxox

About the Author

Kelli McKinney

When Kelli McKinney and her family aren't exploring national parks, she can be found sipping cinnamon tea, struggling to keep houseplants alive, or chucking a toy across the backyard for her English Mastiff. She earned her bachelor's degree in journalism from the University of Oklahoma and her graduate degree in radio/tv/film from the University of North Texas. She enjoyed an eclectic-yet-fulfilling career in corporate marketing before wandering off to be a writer. Now, she is a part-time copywriter, full-time mom, and a children's author. *Jeff Pennant's Field Guide To Raising Happy Parents* is her first book.

* Author Photo Credit Sarah Marie

Chicken Scratch Reading School

JEFF PENNANT'S **Field Guide** TO RAISING HAPPY PARENTS

www.chickenscratchbooks.com/courses

Join us at Chicken Scratch Reading School for your choice of 2 different online Novel Study Courses for *Jeff Pennant's Field Guide To Raising Happy Parents*. Created by certified teachers with extensive curriculum design experience, these offerings are 4 or 6-week courses of study for 4th- 8th grade students. They include reading study focus, interviews, quizzes, vocabulary work, thematic and character analysis, a written essay, and culmination project. The courses include a mix of online and on-paper work, highlighted by instructional videos from the author, Kelli McKinney, and instructor Kiri Jorgensen.

Chicken Scratch Books creates online novel study courses for every book we publish.

Our goal is to teach our readers to appreciate strong new traditional literature.

At Chicken Scratch Books,
Traditional Literature is all we do.

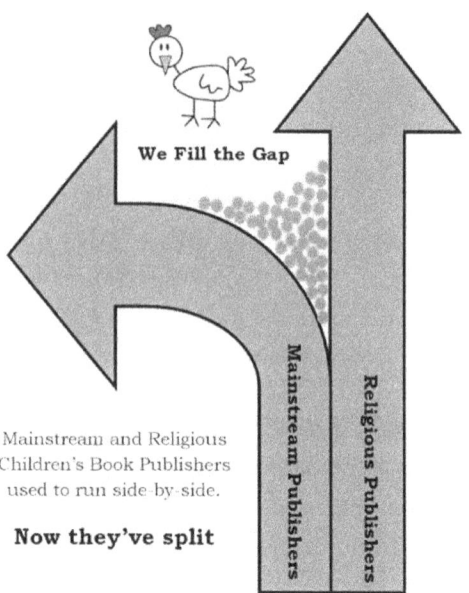

We Fill the Gap

Mainstream Publishers

Religious Publishers

Mainstream and Religious Children's Book Publishers used to run side-by-side.

Now they've split

CPSIA information can be obtained
at www.ICGtesting.com
Printed in the USA
BVHW041301220922
647758BV00003B/660